Being a Minister's Wife... and Being Yourself

Nancy Pannell

BROADMAN PRESS
Nashville, Tennessee

4253-59

ISBN: 0-8054-5359-8

Dewey Decimal Classification: 253.2
Subject Heading: MINISTERS' WIVES
Library of Congress Card Catalog Number: 92-37853
Printed in the United States of America

Unless otherwise stated, all Scripture quotations are from the *New American Standard Bible.* ©The Lockman Foundation, 1960, 1962, 1963, 1968, 1971, 1972, 1973, 1975, 1977. Used by permission.

Scripture quotations marked KJV are from the *King James Version of the Bible.*

Scripture quotation marked TLB are from *The Living Bible.* Copyright © Tyndale House Publishers, Wheaton, Illinois, 1971. Used by permission.

Scripture quotations marked RSV are from the *Revised Standard Version of the Bible,* copyrighted 1946, 1952, © 1971, 1973 by the National Council of Churches of Christ in the U.S.A., and used by permission.

Library of Congress Cataloging-in-Publication Data

Pannell, Nancy, 1936-
    Being a minister's wife . . . and being yourself / Nancy Pannell.
        p.   cm.
    ISBN 0-8054-5359-8
    1. Clergymen's wives. 2. Clergy—Spouses.   I. Title.
BV4395.P357   1992
253' .2—dc20

01   02   03   04   10   9   8   7

To Zack
who is responsible for
my becoming a minister's wife,
and to Mom and Dad,
who have been my greatest fans
since September 1, 1936

Contents

Foreword by Jeannette Clift George

Nancy Pannell has written a delightful book, and I am honored to have the opportunity of writing its foreword. However, I apparently missed the seminar on How-to-Write-a-Foreword and am bewildered by the processing of this opportunity. A writer always hopes he will erase less than he writes, but in this instance that has not been the case. I have written paragraphs on my computer that I dissolved before the sentences were finished. I have glared at the blank screen, challenging it to fill itself with wonderful words... or even moderately sensible words. I have prayed, cried, fussed, and fumed, and eaten countless packages of oatmeal cookies! Now, considering the chocolate pudding in the refrigerator, I have stopped to appraise the reason for my writers' block! It is obvious. I have not been trying to solve the writing assignment, but to figure out who I have to be in order to write a foreword. I have seen myself as inadequate to the task and thus sought some other-than-me person to fulfill it.

That very dilemma is the major address of Nancy Pannell's book *Being a Minister's Wife... and Being Yourself*. She reminds us that God always tailors His instruction for the person receiving it—not for the person who might have been. He may honor us with

His discipline, editing, affirmation, or approval, but He always starts with us as we are. We waste time, talent, energy, and produce when we focus on the fantasy instead of beginning the process in the fact of our identity. When God chooses to change me, He begins with the me He wants to change.

I direct a Christian Theater Company with thirty employees, each of whom is important to me and necessary to this unique ministry. Often I have stood in my hallway calling out a full roster of names trying to get my mind to the right person: "Patty—uh I mean—Elizabeth—Martha!" God never gets us mixed up. The size of His family never confuses Him! He never blurts out *Jeannette* when He meant to call Virginia! The very book that I am trying to foreword, reminds me that whether my copy is used, rewritten, or discarded, my contribution must begin with me. That is true information for the wife, the parent, the minister, and the minister's wife... and Nancy Pannell writes of truth.

Honesty is always more welcome when it wears a smile. Nancy's honesty not only smiles, it giggles, it snickers, and frequently laughs out loud. She says, with charming anecdotes bearing witness, that she was no more prepared for being a minister's wife than I was prepared to write a foreword. She invites us to join in the laughter of her learning and celebrate the teaching of God.

Frequently, dry obedience is doggedly following the path of duty when joy happens! Joy happened to Nancy, and she writes of its divine intrusion in a manner that takes the loneliness out of duty and welcomes God into the routine of obedience. She is a good storyteller with a good story of marriage, of ministry, of growth, and of grace.

I regret the oatmeal cookies and no longer consider the chocolate pudding. Something far more nourishing has been given me. A reminder of God's invitation to enjoy my life and its assignments. To thank Him for love and laughter and to trust Him to set my course. In the Grace of Christ there is room for each of us. Nancy will invite you to celebrate you in the perfect Grace of Christ.

PREFACE

According to Knight's Law, "Life is what happens to you while you are making other plans." What a commentary on my life! It never occurred to me that I would marry a clergyman. I had other plans.

When God surprised me with a minister husband, I loved His choice of mate but questioned His wisdom about the ministry thing. Amazingly, both God and my husband were patient. Now, looking back through thirty-five years of laughter, sorrow, victories, mistakes, disappointments, joy, and crises, I can see God's hand in it all—a hand that not only gently pushed, but also sustained.

My greatest ongoing battle was the conflict between trying to meet perceived expectations and wanting to be simply me. One of God's neatest surprises was the discovery that He wants each of us (even ministers' wives!) to be his or her own unique person.

In recent years an idea began forming, growing in my mind. My thirty-plus years' experience as a minister's wife (and all the vast accumulated wisdom) need not be wasted. I would write a book for church staff wives. One morning at two o'clock I awoke, feverish with excitement and inspiration. The book was all there in my head, bursting to be let out—everything the world has wanted to know—and more—about *The Church Staff Wife*. For days I held forth at the typewriter, certain the institutional church had waited too long for these words.

Then came an unsettling discovery. Many splendid books had already been written for and about ministers' wives. One of the latest, *The Minister's Mate—Two for the Price of One?* even dared beat me to a clever title. Drat!

Can there possibly be a need for even one more such book? Can anything new be said? I believe so! The growing numbers of seminars and retreats for church staff wives underscore the need. Also, old and sometimes forgotten truths can be presented in different packagings. A thought can be expressed from a different perspective, bring new insight to some, fresh encouragement to others.

One limitation with existing books about the minister's wife is the fact they are almost all written by *pastors' wives to pastors' wives*. The number of ordained *non-pastor* ministers has greatly increased. There is a need, I believe, for a book written to and about *all* church staff wives. There are some problems unique to the support staff not faced by the pastor and wife. With growing church staffs, the term "staff wife" is heard as often as "minister's wife." I will use the terms synonymously.

Another problem I have with many books for the minister's wife is the feeling they are presenting an unrealistic view of the proper minister's wife—sort of a combination of Mary Poppins, Marabelle Morgan (the total woman), and Joan of Arc. Nice-sounding advice is given, leaving the impression if we're just spiritual enough or dedicated enough or efficient enough, our problems will be solved. I do not intend to be flippant or critical. I simply know "t'aint" always so. My desire is to share an honest, even if at times painful, journey of one who has struggled—with life *and* the ministry.

Many church staff wives have never labored with their roles. (Or so they say!) Many have walked confidently, joyfully with their mates, dedicated to their calling. Yet I've known many others who privately confided their almost constant frustration with life in the ministry. In conferences I have led, scores of staff wives have voiced feelings ranging from guilt to hostility about their circumstances.

Some wives try to meet perceived expectations, resenting every minute. Some repress their feelings and get sick a lot. Some are outrageously rebellious, trying to shock by nonconformity.

I don't know if crises are more prevalent in ministers' homes today than ever before, or if we are simply more aware of each others' problems. I do know life is more complex for most of us. Life-styles are changing, and these changes are affecting homes of ministers. Most ministers' wives now work outside the home—many are compelled to work. In many instances, even our churches have complicated our lives by filling our every waking moment with activities and programs. We live in a day when divorce is a reality in the lives of many ministers and mates.

No two staff wives, just as no two churches, are alike. I offer no simplistic answers to problems accompanying life in the ministry. Rather, with the hope you might be helped and affirmed, I share a bit of personal pilgrimage with the Lord *and* with one of His ministers.

For all these reasons, I'm back at the typewriter, writing

to church staff wives, their families, and the congregations with whom they serve about a surprising God who continues to surprise me.

With much love (and a little humor that sometimes gets me into trouble),

Nancy Roberts Pannell

1 While I Was Making Other Plans

You have to watch out for God. He can be sneaky. A young woman wishing to chart her own course for life cannot be too careful.

C. S. Lewis said it first. Relating his intense struggle against conversion, he said, "A young man who wishes to remain a sound Atheist cannot be too careful of his reading. There are traps everywhere—God is, if I may say it, very unscrupulous."[1]

And, just as God placed scholarly, credible believers in Lewis's path, God placed a handsome, young minister-to-be in mine. I hadn't planned on being a minister's wife. As a matter of fact, I hadn't planned on being anyone's wife right away. A *free-spirited, independent soul* (I thought), I had ambitious plans.

I would become a successful journalist (perhaps a foreign correspondent for a glamorous magazine) and write probing stories and books. There was room for marriage in my grand plan. But I would marry someone who shared my interests in writing and travel—and who had the money to support them!

God is not only unscrupulous, He has a sense of humor. He no doubt exercised it one day when He looked down on this unsuspecting nineteen-year-old coed at Baylor University and said, "She hasn't attended Sunday night church or a BSU (Baptist Student Union) meeting or a Wednesday night BRH (Baylor Religious Hour) meeting in three years. Wouldn't it be funny if I zapped her into falling in love with a minister and she had to spend the rest of her life going to WMU (Woman's Missionary Union)?"

Can't you just hear my testimony at the annual ministers' wives conference? (You know, those are retreats where ministers' wives get together once a year and "share." We always "share!") Inevitably, at these gatherings I'm seated next to "Mrs. Serenely Together" who felt God's call to marry a minister while at church camp at age thirteen. This is the woman who has walked sweetly and calmly through life with never a burned Sunday roast or a run in her panty hose.

If I told the truth at these retreats, I'd say, "Well, a funny thing happened to me on the way to growing up. I fell in love with a wonderful guy who became a minister and if God had given me any advance warning I would have run like Jonah in the opposite direction."

Lest you think me a pagan or an outright reprobate, I want you to know I was acquainted with God. My pilgrimage with Him had begun in my youth. Growing up on a Texas farm, I had many conversations (arguably, rather one-sided) with God. Often, during those wonderful times of solitude as I rode horseback across the pasture, I talked to Him about my life choices. "Couldn't one be a Christian journalist?" I asked Him. I believed in His program. I just didn't want to be drafted into full-time service.

At Baylor I plunged fervently into a major in journalism, loving the hours I spent at *The Baylor Lariat*, the campus newspaper. Due to my school-teacher dad's insistence, I also worked toward certification in teaching, just in case. And, because I enjoyed music, I joined a choir. The choir president was a good-looking young man (with a beautiful baritone voice) named Zack Parnell.

When I began to feel the undertow toward seminary-bound Zack Pannell, I argued with God, albeit weakly. "Surely, Lord, I'm totally unprepared for the role of minister's wife. Hey, I would never have passed Sunday School if promotion hadn't been based on age."

Zack certainly had ample warnings that I might not be your basic staff wife. The first time he saw me I was hurdling a small hedge in front of Memorial Hall, the sophomore women's dormitory. I was late for class (it was not the last time I would be late for something) and was taking the most direct route. (Nor was it uncommon for me to take the most direct route in everything—such as expressing my opinions.)

Did God make a mistake when He allowed that very-called young man to fall in love with me? Did Zack make a mistake? Could one be a proper minister's wife if she hurdled hedges and preferred wearing jeans and shorts and going barefoot (not to church, but to most other places)? Could one marry a minister, if, deep in her heart, she was envious of other Christian brethren who didn't have to go to church on Sunday nights? (Quite possibly, I'm a Methodist at heart. I've always resented having to go to church on Sunday nights and am certain God did not have Sunday night church on His agenda. If He did, He would have mentioned it in the Bible.) Could one marry a minister if she had a short sitting-down attention span and was allergic to committee meetings?

One can. And one did.

From the beginning of our marriage, I was proud of Zack's calling and committed to being a good wife. Yet, I chafed at the demands of the ministry. Deep inside lurked an uneasy suspicion I had been swept into the ministry by an occasionally mischievous God. I bristled over "having" to spend so much time doing "church things." The resentment grew until it almost consumed me.

During those years, a pious peer said to me, "When God calls a man to the ministry, He also calls the wife. She may not have been listening very well. I've seen many a ministry ruined because the wife wasn't called or wasn't submissive to her call."

At the time I heard those words, my reaction was immediate and unholy. I felt my life was unraveling, twisting away from almost every dream and personal ambition I'd ever possessed—and, to add insult to injury, that lady had the effrontery to suggest I might be hindering my husband's career! What about *my* career? And what if I hadn't been "called"? Mind you, that was before I had come to terms with the concept of a "special call."

The inability to grasp a sense of special calling tormented me for years. I felt defensive and irritated when the subject was discussed. The impression I somehow lacked a divine commission possessed by my peers was crippling. There was little joy in service because I served mainly out of a sense of obligation. I quarreled with Zack over the long hours he spent at church. I sang in the choir, taught Sunday School classes, went to WMU meetings, directed children's choirs, visited prospects, went to zillions of meetings, and felt generally miserable.

Have you ever felt uncertain of your calling or felt that

your ministry was a burden? Are you ever troubled by doubts that you've been called, and hence, that you can be an appropriate staff wife? Have you ever wondered what constitutes a call? Do both husband and wife have to feel a sense of divine calling to the ministry for it to be blessed, for it to be productive? Does the wife's call have to occur at a precise moment in time or can it be a gradual process of coming to understand and accept God's will?

These are not trivial questions to many staff wives. Thoughtful, earnest Christian women have struggled for answers. Why? Because, without a sense of calling to the demands of ministry, we become easily discouraged, we have no joy in service. This is true whether we are staff wives or any person trying to serve the Lord.

Christians believe a call is an appointment to fulfill a specific task. Usually, we associate it with a full-time Christian vocation. If you've been anxious about your call, cease worrying. But read on!

Vexed by doubt of a precise call, *I missed something important.* I overlooked a major truth. *All children of God are called ones!*

Some of us are slow learners. It took me several years to grasp the amazing truth of Hebrews 3:1. "Therefore, holy brethren, partakers of a heavenly calling" (NASB)

I wondered, to whom was the writer speaking? Was he speaking only to pastors and missionaries, or to all believers?

From *The Interpreter's Bible* I found this thought on Hebrews 3:1. "Holy Brethren might be equivalent to 'Christian brethren.' "[2] *All Christians share this calling.* "The writer reminds his people who they are and who Christ is. The word translated holy literally means 'set apart to God in an exclusive sense.' This doctrine is a declaration not so much of right as of responsibility.... *All God's people are consecrated, and whatever their vocation, their service is to him.*... There is power in this thought. What if to *every* Christian,... should come that sense of being set apart which normally comes to a minister in his ordination!"[3] (author's italics).

"All God's people are consecrated.... set apart. Wow! There *is* power in this thought. For me it was liberating power.

I studied again Ephesians 4:1. "I, therefore, the prisoner of the Lord, entreat you to walk in a manner worthy of the calling with which you have been called."

Commenting on this passage, *The Interpreter's Bible* said, " 'The calling to which you have been called"... might be paraphrased 'the place which God has appointed for you in his plan of the ages.' "[4]

Did God have a place for me in His plan of the ages? Did that place and plan continue to unfold when I met Zack Pannell? Were the place and plan constantly in the process of being revealed? I began to realize the answer to all those questions was yes. And my attitude toward ministry and involvement in the local church began to change.

The words of our Lord in John 15:16 took on new meaning. "You did not choose Me, but I chose you, and appointed you, that you should go and bear fruit, and that your fruit should remain."

Those words, also, were written to *all* believers. I, too, had been chosen! What joy and freedom were experienced when I grasped the import of all those verses. As His child, I shared in His calling.

And then, an even greater liberating truth dawned. I

not only was called, but God wanted to use me because I was His child, not just because I was Zack's wife. *I think I must have shouted with excitement and joy when I realized: A minister's wife should be who she is and do what she does because she is a child of God, not because she is a minister's wife!* That is the central message of this chapter, the underlying thesis of this book. A minister's wife can be a real person! She can wear jeans and go barefoot! The important thing is: she is to discover and be the person God has called her to be. She is to be authentic. Real.

Being simply ourselves is not simple. Particularly, for people who are thrust into the public eye. Chapter 4 attempts to address the elusive concept of discovering our real selves.

More and more I understood I had been called to the "ministry" by virtue of the fact I was a Christian. Dr. Herschel Hobbs wrote, "Unfortunately, many Christians have come to think of 'ministry' in terms of those whose vocation is to devote all their time to Christian work. It was a sad day when a distinction was made between clergy and laity. The distinction suggests a division in function and in responsibility that goes beyond the New Testament practice."[5]

I, too, am called to be a minister as is every child of God. How could I have missed such a widely known truth? Or, is it widely known? Apparently, it is not. As a matter of curiosity, I've begun to ask Christians at random, "Do you believe every Christian is a minister? Do you live with the sense of being a minister?" The answers are surprising. Many folk who have been more than nominally involved in church for years say, "No, I don't think of myself as a minister."

If we belong to Him, God has called us *to serve* Him with whatever gifts He has given. The call to Christ is a call to service, whether one is in a full-time Christian vocation or not.

Romans 12 spurs us to action. From *The Living Bible:*

And so, dear brothers, I plead with you to give your bodies to God. Let them be a living sacrifice, holy—the kind he can accept. When you think of what he has done for you, is this too much to ask? God has given each of us the ability to do certain things well. So if God has given you the ability to prophesy, then prophesy whenever you can—as often as your faith is strong enough to receive a message from God. *If your gift is that of serving others, serve them well.* If you are a teacher, do a good job of teaching. . . . If God has given you administrative ability and put you in charge of the work of others, take the responsibility seriously (vv. 1, 6-8, author's italics).

What sheer fun and amazement it is to discover gifts and watch God develop them!

I'll never forget the first time I taught a Sunday School lesson. I was twenty-three years old and scared to death. The setting was Inspiration Point Baptist Church of Fort Worth, the supportive little congregation that Zack served part time during his seminary days. I stood behind a speaker's stand (we thought the teacher was always supposed to stand) before a class of three or four young women. That Sunday, from a study in Genesis, I taught the doctrine of creation, the Trinity, man, sin, and redemption in thirty minutes. Though I did everything wrong, God honored the attempt to serve Him. No doubt, He has smiled many times at my attempts to teach the Bible—such as the time I taught a whole lesson on prayer and never once prayed, before, during, or after.

One of the neatest surprises of life has been finding out God can use me just as I am. Do not misunderstand. I'm not saying we're to be satisfied with our spiritual level and complacent about spiritual growth. But, I am saying when we offer whatever skills and knowledge and personality we have to Him, He does exciting things! I don't have to pretend to be more spiritual than I am. I don't have to pretend to be more intellectual, more efficient, or wiser. I can be me.

Responding to the call of Jesus has led to some unusual experiences and lots of surprises. Chapter 6 records some of those.

God will continue to give us opportunities to serve as long as we're willing, and He will usually even make the serving fun! Whatever gift or gifts He has given you, get busy using them and start having fun. One caution, it's possible to overload. More about that in chapter 4.

It occurs to me that Christian leaders have so emphasized the concept of special calling for full-time Christian work, they have failed to stress the unique calling of every Christian. Who is called? All are called who have responded to God's message of salvation.

Must the minister's wife experience a definite special call, apart from the call inherent in salvation? A minister of education friend responded to my question in a lovely way. He reasoned, "I know God called me into the ministry. My wife and I always figured when God brought us together He was including her in my call. That was His way of calling her!"

A staff wife friend put it this way: "Larry was not in the ministry when we married. I don't think he would ever have responded to God's call if both of us had not felt it was the right direction for our lives."

On the other hand, some staff wives really have felt a unique sense of calling. One wrote in response to a questionnaire, "I felt a special call as a teenager. I believe a sense of special calling on the wife's part helps make the husband and wife more of a team from the beginning."

Still another staff wife wrote, "I've never felt a sense of calling to a full-time Christian vocation. The Lord called my husband to be a minister of music, but I've never felt any different from any other church member. I don't feel the circumstances of life are somehow different for a staff wife, or that my problems are different from other church members. I have always felt like a church member responding to God's call within that local body of believers."

In my case, the call to a full-time Christian vocation was a gradual process of coming to understand and accept God's continuing revelation of His will. He has led me to be a minister's wife and called me, as He has called all believers, to be a minister. But He didn't call me to do Zack's work! I am called to the place which He has appointed me in His plan of the ages, which, interestingly, has blended and harmonized with Zack's calling. The call to minister will never be withdrawn. The place, in the sense of task or role, keeps changing.

The preceding paragraphs show differences in staff wives and in the ways they have interpreted their calling. Yet, all have been used by God because all have grasped the concept that the call to Christ is a call to service. A sense of calling for your task, whatever it is, is a prerequisite to commitment to the task. Without that sense of calling, we are more likely to experience discouragement or burnout.

Being called and given gifts by God does not mean the

task will be easy, or always pleasant. When your husband is a minister, you may on many occasions wonder, "Are we having fun yet?"

The rest of this book is about getting to the fun part and making it through the not-fun parts, whether your husband is the pastor or a part of the team assisting the pastor. It is also for church members who periodically need help in understanding that strange breed—the "staff wife."

Now, when I receive an invitation that reads, "Join us for a ministerial wives' get-together as we celebrate our special calling," I am no longer frustrated or negative. I go and celebrate!

Zack used to quip, "Honey, I love you in spite of, as well as because of." I think that may be an accurate, though gramatically flawed, expression of God's sentiments toward us! He not only loves us in spite of, but uses us in spite of our limitations and lack of understanding when we give our abilities to Him.

I am now able to pray, *Thank You for calling me. Thank you, Father, for loving and using me in spite of. Thank you for Your incredible patience. And, by the way, Lord, thanks for giving me the good sense thirty-five years ago to say yes to both You and Zack Pannell! And, Lord, help me to have a sweeter spirit about going to church on Sunday nights.*

2

God Didn't Know Ministers Were Supposed to Have Perfect Children

The brief note in my hands, printed in her neat script, made me cry. It simply said, "Mom, I know I don't always show it, but I want you to know I really love you."

I came across the note in a drawer where I've placed special cards, clippings, and mementos. The note had come from Carolyn, our daughter, several years ago during her freshman year at college. I probably cried when I first received it; now, tears flowed again as I cherished that meaningful note and as images of Carolyn flashed through my mind—the sunny, lovable little girl playing with her dolls; the conscientious student eager to please her teachers; the dedicated cross-country runner getting up at 5:30 to run three miles before dressing for school; the stormy, restless teenager eager to get away from home; the tall, beautiful young woman, looking both bold and vulnerable, who waved good-bye as she faced the beginning of her freshman year at Baylor.

The note was eloquent. I knew it meant, "Mom, in spite of our misunderstandings, our differences, our times of disappointing each other, I want you to know I really love you." I understood. And I cherished the affirmation, because parenting had not been easy. It never is.

The same drawer contained a newsclipping of Kenny,

our son, at age ten, holding the trophy he'd won in the pass, punt, and kick contest. I smiled, remembering the little boy who was never still, who was always in motion, kicking something, throwing something, climbing something, wrestling someone, teasing someone—usually his little sister.

"There is a time for every event under heaven—A time to weep, and a time to laugh" (Eccl. 3:1,4a).

Surely, this Scripture was written with the minister's family in mind!

If you're normal, you've wondered, "How can I be a spiritual 'All-Pro' mom when my family is *so human?*" When your children aren't saintly (that is, when they turn out to be normal) it helps to laugh a lot.

To the house of Zack and Nancy were added Kenny and Carolyn. Apparently, God did not know ministers' children were supposed to be perfect. He did not give us perfect children. At times I wondered if they would ever even like each other.

As the writer of Ecclesiastes says, the tough times, the weeping times, are inevitable. But they are so much easier to handle when one has cultivated a spirit of laughter and joy. If you are the totally stressed-out woman— whether minister's wife or layperson suffering from hyperactivity at church—this chapter is for you. Understand, there are two times in life when we are experts on rearing children: (1) before we have children and (2) after our children are grown and we have the marvelous benefit, as I do now, of 20/20 hindsight.

Often, during those frenetic years of parenting, the counsel of an older minister friend helped my perspective. "Remember," he once advised Zack and me, "you can never take our Lord's work too seriously. But, be

careful that you don't take yourselves too seriously."
Sometimes, especially with children, not taking ourselves
too seriously is the best response.

It is time to laugh when you are sitting beside a
squirming four-year-old through a long worship service.
He drops a book or pencil for the seventeenth time. You
glare at him and say, "Kenny, I'm sick and tired of this!"
He responds quickly, "I am, too, Mama. Let's go home."

It was time not to take myself seriously when we were
at church and six-year-old Carolyn accidentally knocked
off... well, let me tell you about it. God has the most
capricious ways of humbling us. Neither I nor some of the
members at the First Baptist Church of Muskogee, Oklahoma, are likely to forget that particular Sunday morning—
the morning I wore a wig to church. Remember the days
of the fashion wigs? Remember how appalling one's real
hair looked after being flattened under the wig?

That infamous Sunday Carolyn persuaded me to sit in
the balcony with her. To Carolyn, at age six, ultimate joy
was sitting in the balcony right by the rail. That way,
when we stood to sing or pray, she could lean over and
look down and be both awed and scared by the height.
All went well until the closing prayer. I leaned over
Carolyn to help with her coat. (That's probably when
God got the idea. He knew I was rushing to beat the
crowd down the stairs, instead of listening to the prayer.)
As I struggled with Carolyn's coat while juggling a purse
and Bible, her arm shot upward through a coat sleeve,
caught the edge of my wig and sent that wig sailing
over the balcony rail, airborne like an unidentified fly-
ing varmit, to land unceremoniously on a startled wor-
shiper. In such a time, one has a choice, to weep, to
destroy a kid, or to laugh. I laughed hysterically, like a

demented woman, all the way home, after setting a new track record out of the church. Curious thing about that incident. Moments before, I was feeling particularly impressed with my spirituality, with all I was doing to serve the Lord.

If there's any justice in the world, however, I will be allowed to live long enough to see my children become parents of teenagers. During one five-year span, our two teenagers collectively had six car wrecks, had to be rushed to the hospital emergency several times (once after showing off at the swimming pool diving board), got lost in a blizzard on a mountain in Colorado, drove a motorcycle into a brick wall before finding out the throttle was not the brake lever.

Toward the end of those turbulent years, Carolyn was leaving for an eight-hour drive to college. After saying our good-byes, I added, "Be sure to telephone us the minute you get there."

I'll never forget her words. "Mom, I wish you would lighten up. I don't know why you worry so much."

At the moment, I wanted to smack her. Actually, though, her words were biblical—sort of a loose paraphrase of Philippians 4:16 (if you don't know it, look it up!). Although she couldn't understand a mother's concern and be properly empathetic, her advice to lighten up was good counsel.

Many harsh words, tears, and frustrations could have been avoided if I had earlier relaxed and laughed more. Thank heavens, before my children were grown, I did learn it's OK for a minister's children to be normal. And normal children are often less than saintly.

Normal parents make mistakes, too. One of my least damaging mistakes was the time I misunderstood my little daughter's question. Carolyn was barely six. The year was 1968—back in the Dark Ages when females wore bathing caps at public swimming pools. Carolyn had gone swimming with a neighbor and her children. When she got home, Carolyn came into the kitchen where I was cooking our evening meal and very seriously asked, "Mom, what's the difference between boys and girls?"

I gulped. The time had obviously come. I wasn't prepared for an in-depth discussion on sex with my little daughter quite yet, but, being a modern young mother, I wanted to do the right thing at the right time. I literally put everything on the back burner, and took a deep breath and went into the den with Carolyn for our first serious mother/daughter talk. I was as honest as I knew how to be with a six-year-old. I talked for at least twenty minutes. Her little face gazed into mine with rapt interest. Finally, I finished and I added, "Now, Honey, if there's anything you don't understand or want to ask me, go ahead. You can always ask me anything. Is there anything else you want to know?"

She sort of shrugged her little shoulders and said, "No. I was just wondering why girls have to wear bathing caps at the swimming pool and boys don't."

It is not only helpful to recognize that we and our children are normal human beings, it is imperative to learn to slow down, to say no to outside forces vying for our time. Even when those forces are Christian. When our children were young, my perception of "how children of the church staff should behave" and my anxiety about "what people in the church will think" made me too rigid. I allowed well-meaning, but legalistic, people to lay guilt trips on me. And I passed them on to my children.

Once a fellow staff wife took me to task for not joining WMU. At the time, I was teaching public school (to put hubby through seminary) and leaving my toddler five days a week with a sitter. Our little son was also being left at the church nursery twice every Sunday, most Monday evenings, while I made visits with my husband, and every Wednesday evening. I tried to explain, "My baby is being left with others too much right now. When he gets older and I'm not working full time, I'm going to join your group."

The woman's response was caustic.

"The Lord is not interested in what you're *going to do*. He is concerned about what you are *not* doing right now." In a way, she was right. She had not intended a double message, but the Lord was concerned about what I was *not* doing. I was not spending appropriate time with my child.

Gradually, I not only learned to lighten up, I learned the children and I did not have to be at every church-sponsored activity, at every meeting. God, Zack, and my mother convinced me the sun would still rise in the east if the children and I missed an occasional service at church. Nevertheless, I collected much needless guilt, even when common sense told me we needed to stay home.

Our son, who is now a daddy, said to me, "My memories of going to church on Sunday are good, but I hated Wednesdays. All I can remember about Wednesdays is how tense and tired we all were by the time we got home that night. The minute we kids got home from school, you were rushing us off to children's choir. On Wednesdays you always seemed anxious about all the things you were trying to do. You were either playing the piano for one of our children's choirs or directing one of them.

After eating supper at church and going to prayer meeting, we kids had mission activities and you went to adult choir practice. We usually got home about ten o'clock and still had homework to do. I dreaded Wednesdays."

Ken's words are an indictment of many Christian parents *and of our perception of what pleases the Lord.* Ephesians 5:10 tells us, "Learn as you go along what pleases the Lord" (TLB).

Of course it pleases the Lord for us to serve Him, but He didn't ask us to do it all on Wednesday nights! He didn't tell us, either, the only way to serve Him was at church. Why do you suppose we have equated spirituality with much busyness at church?

I would not be misunderstood about the importance of worshiping together as family. Corporate worship has been the catalyst that brought unity and stability and strength to our family. The local body of believers where I belong and worship is very dear. But there are many ways of serving Christ in addition to service through the local church. May I suggest one of the greatest and most challenging ways to serve Him is to become the best wife and mother you can be. That way involves gaining the wisdom to know when to stay home, when to say no even to good causes.

Inadvertently, we in the ministry (and many other religious persons) often do our children a great injustice by trying to "cram church" down them much as we pour medicine down them when they are sick. "Here! Take this. It will make you be sweet and do good." The end result may be a child who becomes blatantly rebellious. Of course we could never overexpose our children to Christ, to Christlike attitudes, integrity, and actions; but we can overexpose them to "religious activity." Be honest. Do you have unrealistic expectations of your children, particularly in the area of religious activity? Are you expecting them to be models of near-perfect children? Is your rigidity driving your children away from God (so that the minute they leave home, they abandon church), or are you turning them into young Pharisees (young people who are known to their peers primarily by what they are *against*)? I have come to believe that we who are active in church are more prone toward the tendency of rigidity than laxness and leniency.

What *is* too rigid? I believe we are being too rigid when we are more concerned about "what people think" than we are about the needs of our children. Zack and I both plead guilty on this charge during our early years of parenting. Sadly, I recall the time we forced our shy, five-year-old son to sing in a church music program and his anxiety made him physically ill.

We are being too rigid when our children feel they are loved conditionally, loved only when they "keep the rules," when they are good, and when they meet our expectations. No normal, caring parent intends to communicate *conditional* love. Yet most of us sometimes fall into the trap of communicating conditional love, usually when we are tired and frustrated. To my sorrow, I can remember making such remarks as, "Why are you so bad?" or "Why can't you be more neat or polite (etc.), like your sister (brother)?" Or "God will punish you when you act like that." Those are messages of conditional love.

We are being too rigid when we criticize and find fault more than we praise and encourage. Every child is vulnerable and in constant need of affirmation. I believe we are being too rigid when we make our children feel they must excel in whatever they attempt. Likely, we want them to excel at "being ministers' children!" It is easy for us parents to unwittingly pressure our children to excel, even in areas where they may not be exceptional, such as academic or sports achievements, because we are basing our self-esteem on their accomplishments.

We are being too rigid, I believe, if we always make our children put church activities before other activities. Note that I said "church activities," not the Lord! A colleague of Zack's once boasted that he had never allowed his teenage son to play in a school ball game on a Wednesday night. The staff member said, "We taught our son that he was to be at church on Wednesday nights and we told his coaches that if they scheduled games on Wednesday nights our son wouldn't be there." *When,* I wondered, did *Wednesday night become sacred?* Why must we be so rigid that we often make our children rebel against the very One we want them to love.

Indeed, rearing children requires the greatest of all wisdom! Too often I was unwise, but a promise I began to claim over and over again is found in James 1:5, "But if any of you lacks wisdom, let him ask of God, who gives to all men generously and without reproach, and it will be given to him."

Note the word "generously." God is always ready to give us abundant wisdom when we ask for the right reasons.

The writer of Proverbs has something to say to us mothers. "She looks well to the ways of her household. . . . Her children rise up and bless her; her husband also." (Prov. 31:27-28).

Actually, I identify most with the haggard wife and mother who said she could hardly get her children to rise up, much less bless her. Nevertheless, Proverbs gives us good advice. How do we manage to have the wisdom to "look well to the ways of our household"? Verse 30 gives the answer. It says that an excellent wife and mother is one "who fears the Lord."

Surely, the most important thing we can do as mothers is to seek guidance from the Lord. I cannot imagine surviving the stress of parenting without a growing personal relationship with the Lord. I wish I could say I always started the day with a quiet time of prayer and Bible study. But I would be the world's greatest fraud if I did. Probably, I have begun and forsaken more attempts at a daily quiet time than any other child of God. Yet from the day each of my children was born, I have committed each child to Him and lived with a consciousness of dependence on Him. I have attempted to practice His presence, often praying while driving to and from work, often snatching moments of the day for dialogue with Him.

We can have a beautiful prayer life, refrain from over-extending ourselves at church, have a terrific sense of humor, and still miss a major essential in parenting. We can miss getting to know these wonderful creations, our children. Getting to know them takes time (when we may want to do something else) and effort. Do you really know who your children are? Do your children know who you are? Do you really know what they think and how they feel?

Recently, I asked Zack what he would do differently as a father if he could go back thirty years. He said, "I would spend more time with my family. From the beginning, I would plan a weekly time to be with my family away from church and guard that time jealously."

It is amazing how many Christian parents our age say the same thing. Admittedly, the sheer reality of economics forces many women to work outside the home. Many women don't have the option of staying home. But if you have to work outside the home, you can choose how you spend the rest of your time. Prayfully consider how you use your time, and begin to make time with your children one of your highest priorities. You say, "Fine. I agree that we should do this. But how? You know the demands on a minister and his wife!"

Just plan for it and do it. Ministers aren't the only ones who have trouble finding time to spend with family. Zack eventually began the practice of taking at least half a day off every week and making certain he spent at least one evening a week with family. Let your children help plan the use of this time. Sometimes strange and interesting evenings result! You may find yourself having a picnic in the middle of the living room floor, or you may be treated to a meal of peanut butter and jelly sandwiches and fruit-flavored punch prepared by the children.

Celebrate family! Most of the best times were when our family was alone together. Out of those moments grew our special traditions, our inside jokes, our ability to love and accept each other in spite of human fallibilities.

One of the most unique times we ever shared as family was the Sunday night we *didn't* go to church! (A minister's family did what?) Zack was on vacation, but we were spending it at home, not out of town. He had just come through an extraordinarily busy time, a time during which he had hardly seen his teenage son and eleven-year-old daughter. On Sunday morning we went to church as usual, not even thinking of doing otherwise. But, late that afternoon, as church time approached, Kenny said, "Dad, I wish we could just stay home together tonight."

I can't know all that went through Zack's mind in that moment, but his answer was surprising. "Tell you what," he said, "it's a beautiful afternoon. Let's get Mom to pack a picnic supper and we'll all go out to the farm where Bo stays. (Bo was Kenny's horse, farmed out on the property of friends.) We'll build a camp fire and roast weiners and have our own worship service out there."

That's exactly what we did. After eating, we sat around the fire and sang choruses. Zack asked each of us to tell something we were thankful for or to relate some answered prayer. We prayed together. We laughed when Bo came up in the dark and nudged Kenny from behind, almost knocking him into the fire. We watched the first stars come out. It was an experience for which I'll always be thankful! The cows and horses that grazed nearby may never be the same! Some may even have made a decision to become Baptists that night!

Granted, hindsight is much clearer than foresight. I can look back at this stage in life and see the things both wise and foolish we did. Recognizing that every family's interests, opportunities, and personalities are different, I still want to share some reflections. Possibly you will find them helpful if you are in that wonderful stage of The Full (or Partially Full) Nest. *I'm glad we:*

- took many planned vacations even when money was scarce, which it always was! From swimming at the beach to trout fishing in Colorado, we logged more than our fair share of sand, sunburn, and mosquito bites.
- went on all those Friday night-Saturday camping trips. The old tent, lantern, and cookstove in the attic

are happy reminders of evenings around campfires at Lake Tenkiller.

* invested money in Patches, the mare, and spent all those hours (even in below-freezing temperatures) riding, feeding, and caring for her. Our children learned much about responsibility during the four years we had Patches and her surprise colt, Bo.
* made the effort to arrange for Carolyn to ride Patches in the Fourth of July parade, even though it meant breaking the city ordinance by keeping a horse in the backyard the night before the parade.
* went to all of Kenny's Little League games, basketball games, football games, and band concerts.
* went to all of Carolyn's piano recitals, plays, track meets, and band concerts.
* let out teenage son grow long hair even though he looked like a shaggy dog and some church members were critical. Length of hair is not a test of faith.
* were supportive and uncritical of our teenage daughter during her three car wrecks in an eighteen-month period. Two of them really weren't her fault!

I wish we had not:

* ever said, "Not now. I'm too busy," when either of our children asked us to read them a story.
* been so preoccupied we were not tuned in to our preteen daughter's silent pleas for attention and help. I know, now, that meeting the needs of our children is far more important than a clean house or a job or a meeting.
* forced our son to sing in church choir all those years when he hated it so much. Being in choir is not a prerequisite for heaven.
* ever made our children feel a certain behavior was

expected of them *because their dad was on church staff.*

I wish we had:

- been more consistent in maintaining family devotionals. Believe it or not, this may be harder for church staff families than for others. So much time is spent at church in worship and Bible study, we may tend to neglect this important responsibility.
- preached less and listened more. Listening to our children, accepting them, and loving them unconditionally does not mean condoning and agreeing with their behavior.
- understood that the healthy family is one where each member (including children) is encouraged to express feelings and needs, where each feels "safe."

We began this chapter by quoting Ecclesiastes 3:4. To paraphrase and amplify that verse, "There is a time to cry together and a time to lighten up, there is a time to discipline and a time to support, there is a time to advise and a time to listen, there is a time to set limits and a time to turn loose."

Turning loose is the hardest part. As we began to turn loose, our children made some mistakes. They, *like we,* made some bad choices, didn't always use good judgment. Turning loose means allowing our children to fail—while maintaining steadfast love.

Our family has not gone unscathed by crises. We know what it is to sit all night by the telephone, waiting, praying, not knowing where that teenage son or daughter is, feeling paralyzed by fear. We know what it is to walk with a grown son or daughter through the agonizing grief of divorce. We know what it is to get that ominous telephone call in the middle of the night telling us that one of our children is in the intensive care unit at the hospital. We know what it is to drive to the hospital with fear so numbing we don't know how to pray any prayer except "Lord, help our child. Please help our child."

The important thing is, we have weathered the bad times together, *as family.* We have come to understand we are human. Such understanding helps us reach out to minister to others. Such understanding rips away a spirit of condemnation.

Being in the ministry—being Christian—does not mean our families will be free of problems. Some of the most godly Christians I've known have suffered deep anguish because of problems with children. Christian families today are walking through the valleys of divorce, suicide, alcoholism and drug abuse, and prison terms. We often don't know or understand why.

But the Christlike family keeps on loving. The Christlike family forgives and does not sit in judgment. The Christian family apologizes when it is appropriate. It isn't easy for parents to say to their children, "I was wrong. I'm sorry." On many occasions I've needed to apologize to my children. Being human, we parents sometimes overreact, misunderstand, speak cuttingly. (How wonderful it would be if the church family, indeed, the larger family of God, could learn and practice the principles of forgiving and seeking forgiveness.)

In spite of all the warts it may have, celebrate family!

At the recent wedding of a young friend, the mother of the bride tearfully said, "I don't know what I'm going to do. I'm not ready to give Lisa up." I've got news for her! We don't "give them up." They keep coming back! Our families just get bigger and bigger.

To the house of Zack and Nancy came other children, Anne and Jeff. (Let me clarify. They didn't move in with us. They married into the clan.) And then our amazing God topped all His creative acts by presenting us Amy Anne Pannell, our first grandchild. Incredibly, He matched that miracle three years later with the gift of Molly Lauren Pannell!

The day Amy was born my devotional reading was Psalm 92. I came upon this verse moments after she was born: "For Thou, O Lord, hast made me glad by what Thou hast done. I will sing for joy at the works of Thy hands" (v. 4).

Since that day of celebration, that verse has become a song of praise and thanksgiving for *all* our children— though, at times, they are still unsaintly.

I'm convinced God gives us grandchildren so that we can have a second chance—a second chance to simply relax and enjoy these amazing little persons called children. Amy and Molly have brought indescribable joy into our lives and have taught us much about life, as did Kenny and Carolyn.

"The Girls," as I usually refer to Amy and Molly, spend a lot of time with us since they live less than two hours away. Of course, I've embraced grandmothering with considerable zeal, striving to be the perfect grandmother, and I had even, for a while, come to think of myself as the wonderful, fun-to-be-with-but-also-saintly grandmother who would always be remembered by her granddaughters. I'll probably be remembered all right, but not as saintly.

Amy was four years old when she found out that her grandmother was flawed. Though delighted on that day to have my little granddaughter visit us, I had had a particularly stressful morning. It was not Amy's fault. There had been countless interrupting telephone calls as I tried to get Amy and myself dressed for a meeting I had to attend. About to be late, I was rushed and anxious. I finally got us both in the car, buckled in, and was starting to back out of the garage when I realized I didn't have my purse. "Oh, *poop*," I exclaimed, and could instantly have ripped out my tongue.

"Nana," came the rebuking little voice from the seat beside me. "Why did you say, *'poop'*?"

I was mortified, as well I should have been. There I was, the Christian grandmother, minister's wife, etc., and I had said something like that in front of a precious, impressionable child.

"Oh, Honey," I said, suffused with guilt, "Nana is so sorry. I should not have said that. I won't ever say that again."

She wasn't about to let me off the hook. "I'll have to tell my mother," she said. And she did. That was the first thing she reported when I took her home three days later.

Recently the girls, now ages six and three, were running helter-skelter through the house, making enough noise to "wake the dead" as my grandmother used to say. I suggested they might be a little quieter. "Nana," said Amy, "You wouldn't be so nervous if you didn't drink so much coffee."

Both girls are trying to straighten me out. My latest "boo-boo" made quite an impression on them. When they learned I had backed our car into (and partially through) our garage door, they were fascinated and eager to see the demolished door. They got to come for a visit before we replaced the door. Molly inspected the hole in the garage door with great interest, then shared some three-year-old wisdom with me. "If you ever back into the garage door again, I guess we'll have to get a new Nana."

Celebrate family!

Lord, thank You for Ken and Carolyn and for the joyful times You've continued to give us together. Thank You for Anne and Jeff, the children You've added to our family. And, Lord, since You didn't see fit to give us perfect children, thank You for giving us perfect grandchildren!

3   For a Good Time...

The impulsive thought hit me as I was leaving church on a warm spring evening. Maybe the fact that it was spring had something to do with it. Wednesday night activities were winding down that evening at First Baptist, Tulsa, Oklahoma, and, having discharged my churchly obligations once more after teaching school all day, I was looking forward to the rest of the evening at home.

En route to my car, I had the impulsive thought. Feeling playful and romantic, I decided to leave a note under the windshield wipers of Zack's car. As usual, we were at church in separate cars. His little red car shouldn't be hard to find, since I knew the area of the church parking lot where he usually parked.

The only paper to be found in my purse was the check book; so I ripped out a deposit slip and on the back of it wrote: "For a good time, call 481-1910 (our home telephone number)." Smiling expectantly, I found the little red car and tucked the note in a prominent place.

As I drove out of the parking lot, I sighted Zack leaving church. I slowed to watch through my rear view mirror, wanting to make sure he found the note. To my horror, he walked past the little red car, went to a different little red car, got in, and drove off. (I've never been able to distinguish one car from another. If two cars are the same color and have four wheels, they look alike to me.)

Right there, in front of God and all the people exiting First Baptist Church, I whipped a U-turn in downtown Tulsa and probably burned rubber getting back to somebody's little red car. I leaped from my car with its engine running, and before the amazed eyes of several approaching church members, grabbed the incriminating note.

My face burned as I drove home. I didn't know whether to laugh or cry over what might have resulted. I didn't know whether or not I should even tell Zack of my latest "near disaster." But one thing I knew—someone from that church would never know what a good time he missed!

Living with me has not been easy. I try to stay out of trouble, but...

Just as there were times I wondered if my children would ever like each other, at times I *knew* Zack and I didn't like each other! Not only can a minister's wife be occasionally unspiritual (sometimes downright cranky), even a minister is not always ministerial at home. He may even be thoroughly disagreeable.

Zack and I are living proof that opposites attract.

He is neat and organized and logical. I am, ... well, you get the picture. To me, the house is neat if we can walk through it and find the most important things—the grandkids, the dog, the refrigerator.

Zack is hot-natured; I am always cold. The miracle of our marriage is its survival of the continuing battle of the thermostat. He turns it down. I turn it up. He says, "Wear a sweater." What I say is unprintable.

I love pets and would turn our home into more of a zoo than it already is. Zack tolerates them, though not always with a sweet spirit.

He likes licorice; I like broccoli.

In recent years we both took a personality test and learned what we already knew—that we were different! That particular test revealed Zack to be a fairly high "C" personality—someone who is very controlled and orderly, someone who wants everything in its place and knows where everything is. You've already guessed. I registered as a fairly high-type "I" personality. We "I's" are the ones who don't know where *anything* is, . . . and couldn't care less!

Recently I was reminded again of our differences. We were preparing for a Christmas open house to which more than seventy had been invited. There *are* a few occasions when I *do* care about what the house looks like, and that was one of them. Late in the afternoon of The Day, as I frantically ran in circles to complete last-minute details, Zack felt a holy calling to clean out and reorganize the kitchen pantry. Though I pointedly suggested there were higher priorities on our work list—such as preparing food trays, building a fire, bringing in extra chairs—he remained oblivious to my remarks. In fact, he found his project so satisfying, he started on an even higher calling—the back bedroom closet. By the time the guests arrived, I was hostile. As Zack serenely surveyed the neatly stacked canned goods and the orderly row of boxes in the pantry, he said, "I don't know why you get so uptight about these affairs. Why can't you just relax and enjoy having people over?"

Acts of violence do cross my mind.

And, in all fairness, I must admit Zack has had justifiable cause for violence, too! Living with me would have tested even the patience of Saint Paul. If I back through our garage door one more time, Zack will kill me and the jury will acquit him. Actually, I've backed into it twice. The first time wasn't so bad. A hundred-dollar visit by the garage door repairman put the old door back in usable condition. But the last time... How do you explain jumping into your car (not just once, but twice) and backing out without ever looking behind you? (My Christmas gift that year was a five-hundred dollar, new, insulated, steel garage door—just what I'd always wanted.)

My tone has been light, but my message is serious. The marriage of two Christians is not at all times Christian. Ministers and mates have marriage problems, too. To pretend otherwise is gross hypocrisy. Today, divorce is touching more ministers' families than ever before. The reasons are many and complex. Part of the reason, no doubt, is some wives' perceptions and misconceptions of their roles (as ministers' wives), causing anxiety and resentments that cripple the marriage. Part of the reason may lie in the fact that many ministers give themselves so totally to their work that they neglect and fail their own families.

We live in a day when many wives of ministers work outside the home. As I've already stated, many are forced to work for economic reasons. Many women feel led into various careers and professions. New problems arise in any marriage when both husband and wife work full time outside the home, particularly when there are children at home. Problems are compounded when one is forced to bear the major responsibilities of parenting. Problems are further compounded when one is on a church staff and both have endless responsibilities at church.

Pressure on the working wife is increased if her husband is not inclined to help at home. The pressure on the wife who works outside the home and maintains the home single-handedly can be almost unbearable. The pressure is intensified by uncharitable attitudes of church members. Recently I overheard this remark, "It's such a pity our pastor's wife wants to work. It prevents her attending our Sunday School class parties and our mission group." It evidently never crossed the mind of the speaker that her pastor's wife might:

    a.) have to work for economic reasons;

    b.) be making a significant contribution to society through her work;

    c.) be finding in her work an outlet (therapy, if you please) to prevent burnout in the ministry; or

    d.) all of the above!

My claim as a voice of credibility on the subject of marriage is based on the fact I'm a happy survivor of a thirty-five-year marriage. Note, the adjective *happy* is placed before survivor, not before marriage! We laugh at the joke, "I've been happily married for twenty years—and that ain't bad out of thirty years of marriage!" There's more truth than humor in the joke, however.

Isn't it about time a minister's wife talks honestly about marriage? At least one already has. Elain Herrin, in her book *When We Say Never,*[1] is refreshingly open as she tells how she and her husband worked through a painful time, one that could have led to divorce.

Undoubtedly, there are staff wives who feel discouraged, wornout, unappreciated, who feel their marriage has gone stale, who feel inadequate, perhaps even a failure, as a wife—particularly in view of their lofty calling. Many are afraid to seek help or confide in anyone because "everyone knows if you'll just pray about it and get your heart right, your problems will be solved."

I would not minimize the power of prayer; but sometimes we can find ourselves in situations so overwhelming we don't know how to pray. This is addressed specifically in chapter 8.

If your marriage is troubled or even just afflicted by The Ho-Hums, do I have a word of encouragement for you! First, take comfort in the knowledge you are not the only Christian woman or minister's wife with marriage problems. Your mate's calling to Christian ministry does not guarantee marital bliss or exemption from misunderstandings. Let's get real. Christian or not, called or not, you and your mate are two human beings who will at times be angry and depressed, and will at times hurt each other. That's human. It helps to accept your humanity.

Remember, it takes two to make the relationship whole, but only one to break the relationship.

Which brings me to say that there is a subtle, but disturbing message in some books and seminars for ministers' wives. The image is projected of the ideal wife as an ever-smiling woman who constantly nurtures her saintly husband, never thinking of self. (We women are sometimes too inclined to assume the martyr posture. It's unfortunate that some respected voices are leading us farther down that road.) In some quarters, *the burden of responsibility for a happy home* is placed squarely on the shoulders of the wife. The message is we wives are to devote our lives to creating a haven of bliss at home for our pressured, weary clergymen husbands. One pastor's wife suggests we are never to bring up stressful subjects at home for conversation. Admittedly, there have been plenty of times I've hated to bring up stressful subjects— such as the time I got a speeding ticket and had to pay a seventy-five dollar fine! And, yes, there may be some stressful subjects you should not address unless absolutely necessary, such as how much you spent on that drill-team uniform for your daughter—the uniform, without which, her life would have been forever shattered. Some books seem to imply we wives are to single-handedly organize and manage the perfect home.

At the risk of being labeled a heretic (or worse yet, a feminist!), I'm going to be bold. The husband, too, has mutual responsibility for the marriage relationship, for nurturing his mate and for keeping the home running smoothly. Wives get weary, too. Wives also have needs.

It takes two to make the relationship whole.

Many pastors' wives quoted in print tell us we should make our husband our number one priority (other than the Lord). I agree! But they stop too soon. In the healthiest and happiest relationships, *both* husband and wife make each other the number one priority, except for, of course, the Lord.

If I've touched upon something you feel is a problem area in your marriage, perhaps you need to do some honest, loving, *Christian* confrontation with your mate.

I can already hear the rumblings! This writer doesn't sound like a submissive wife! Whether intentional or not, some group has done a number on us, planting the notion that the biblical concept of submission means, among other things, never confronting. We can lovingly and gently express our feelings without attacking our mate. In a healthy marriage, both partners express their needs and feelings.

The concept of the submissive wife has been loudly trumpeted while the biblical teaching of mutual submission of all believers has been almost overlooked in many quarters. Many godly, scholarly Christians believe the Bible teaches mutual responsibility and mutual submission within marriage. Philippians 2:4 says, "Do not merely look out for your own personal interests, but also for the interests of others."

Ephesians 5:21, which certainly includes husbands and wives in its exhortation, says,

"Be subject to one another in the fear of Christ."

Dr. Richard J. Foster, well-known Quaker writer, teacher, and theologian, has written a great deal on the discipline of submission. He believes, "Scripture is not attempting to set forth a series of hierarchical relationships but to communicate to us an inner attitude of mutual subordination. . . . In submission we are at last free to value other people. Their dreams and plans become important to us."[2] He also writes, "Freely and graciously the members of the family make allowances for each other. The primary deed of submission is a commitment to listen to the other family members. Its corollary is a willingness to share, which is itself a work of submission."[3]

Misinterpreting the biblical teaching of submission can be very destructive. Using the teaching of submission to instill feelings of low self-worth or to teach passive acceptance of abuse, which includes verbal put-downs as well as physical abuse, is a gross misunderstanding of the Scripture.

Healing can come from honest, loving confrontation—"speaking the truth in love" (Eph. 4:15). The key words are, of course, "in love." Confronting in love can have wonderful results. It's not ever easy to confront a loved one, but Zack and I are learning some simple techniques that work. We try never to attack the other, but to explain how his or her actions and attitudes make us feel. ("Honey, when you stare at the television or newspaper while I'm talking, I feel like I'm not important to you. You may be hearing me, but I can't tell if you're listening or not.")

We've also learned that some things can, and probably should, simply be overlooked! Dr. Foster's statement, *Freely and graciously the members of the family make allowances for each other*, is a concept worth pondering. Making allowances for the limitations and little irritations of others seems to be missing in many Christian marriages. We fall in love with someone just the way they are, then spend the rest of our lives trying to change them! We say or think things like: "Why can't he be more romantic like Peg's husband?" "Why doesn't she dress more femininely, lose weight, et cetera, and so forth."

I sense an absence in many marriages of something I've come to call "graciousness." We began to lose it, I think, during the decade of the seventies. During that era, a trend became very popular that crushed many marriages. It was the trend of flippant, "put-down" speech. The more clever one became at this kind of speech, the more laughs one drew in public; the victim of the "put-down" seldom laughed. It became very chic to put down your mate (or your children or your parents), disguising it as a joke. The eighties will be remembered as the decade of raised consciousness concerning self-discovery and honesty in relationships. Though I strongly endorse "being our own selves" and being honest about feelings, I keep having the strong belief we have failed to *balance* these concepts with plain, old-fashioned courtesy. Have the words *tolerance* and *acceptance* disappeared from our enlightened vocabularies? I find a missing ingredient in so many books and articles and seminars and groups dealing with all kinds of relationships. I call that missing ingredient "graciousness." I'm not suggesting we ignore destructive behavior or repress feelings. I am suggesting we temper honesty with love, respect, courtesy. "Graciousness" is not quick to point out faults, does not put down, accepts and tolerates the little irritations (recognizing we all are imperfect), and is thoughtful.

One may give mental assent to these concepts yet still struggle in the practical application. What about, for instance, the ongoing war between the sexes over housework?

When it is necessary or mutually agreed upon for the wife to work outside the home, the wife should not bear the homemaking burden alone. (Even when the wife doesn't work outside the home, but has been home all day, working, coping with children, it is neither unmanly nor unministerial for the minister husband to help with the housework!) It is possible for a minister to be faithful to his calling, to serve his church well, and also be a co-laborer at home.

Mary E. Bess, in her book *Tips for Ministers and Mates*, puts it this way: "Shared responsibility is the answer to unorganized confusion."[4] She goes on to insist *every* family member, including the husband, should share household chores, and the husband should share parenting obligations.

For twenty-five years I was a school teacher, rising many mornings at 5:30 and working many nights until very late. Zack encouraged me to teach. I could try to spiritualize my career and say I felt a strong calling to be a Christian teacher in public schools. (That *is* a worthy desire, and eventually I did reach that conclusion about my work.) However, our decision for me to teach school was primarily for financial reasons. The point is, the decision for me to work was *mutual*.

For many years, some of our greatest conflict arose out of divergent concepts of who should do what at home. There were many times of confrontation. Through those rough times of disagreement and working toward solutions, we learned a lot about communication, and we discovered ways to simplify our lives. We discovered what really needed to be done and ways of getting the job done together. But that didn't happen overnight. Zack learned how to vacuum, how to clean the bathroom, and how to shop for groceries—although he did come home once with eight cans of pumpkin because they were on sale. In the midst of teaching and grading papers, cooking meals, and chauffeuring kids all over town, I learned how to balance the checkbook and how not to run out of gas. (The kids helped, too, but this chapter is about marriage, not parenting.)

Our marriage pilgrimage has undergone ups and downs much akin to our individual spiritual pilgrimages. Zack supports my desire to share some of our difficult times, believing it might be helpful to others in similar circumstances.

I am married to a man who has not found it easy to be open and communicative. By nature Zack is nonconfrontational and very controlled. He would rather avoid discussion of things controversial. Early in our marriage he refused to discuss any kind of problem in our relationship, choosing a few times even to walk out the door to avoid an argument.

In those early years, Zack tended to be a workaholic (a common disease of ministers, it seems), spending six to seven long days a week at church. When he came home at night, he was too tired to talk or listen. With two small children, I was teaching school, coming home to do all the housework and most of the parenting, and trying to be involved at church. I was exhausted. Zack and I were rarely alone together. Predictably, we were both unhappy.

I tried to tell him of my growing despair. He replied, "If our marriage has a problem, it's *your* problem. I don't have any problems with it."

One day, in desperation, I telephoned his secretary and made an appointment to see him. I asked her not to reveal my identity. At the appointed time I walked into his office (much to his surprise), sat down across from him, and said, "Honey, we've got to talk. I am officially on your schedule for the next thirty minutes. Will you give me the same attention and concern you would give anyone else who came to you for help?"

He gave me more than thirty minutes! That one experience of honest, loving, Christian confrontation did not immediately and miraculously solve all our problems, but it did prove to be a turning point toward improved understanding.

On other occasions Zack has needed to confront me.

Not so many years ago I became so caught up in mothering a teenage daughter, in work at school, home, and church, in perpetual activity, I lost all joy. Due to my own choices, I was running constantly but resenting every minute of it. I turned into a negative, complaining, self-pitying woman. One day, after I had unleashed a torrent of sharp words, Zack gently said, "Hon, you're not any fun anymore."

His words stung. I felt angry and defensive. I wanted to cry out, "If you had to do all I have to do..."

But deep inside, I knew he was right. I had lost the spirit of laughter and joy. I had forgotten how important it was for us, just the two of us, to play together, to have fun together.

Playing together, as well as praying together, has kept us together! Friends and family members have teased us about our "second honeymoons," but that's all right. Our special dates have ranged from an elaborate night out on the town to simple picnics in the living room in front of the fireplace to spontaneous decisions to take in an afternoon movie. Now, we make certain we plan and follow through with fun times for just the two of us. Discovering new common interests has become an adventure. At middle age, we discovered a mutual interest in "junking around" at flea markets. (Be advised, however, this interest can become addictive and costly!)

How fortunate for me, *for us*, that Zack and I both recognized years ago our mutual responsibility for the success of our marriage. From the beginning, our two independent personalities have had to work at making our marriage work. Thank the Lord we've known that what we had together was worth the effort to keep it together!

And it does require effort. It is puzzling that we Christians will work so conscientiously at everything else to which we're committed, yet often neglect working at marriage. We hear and read a lot about commitment. Commitment is not just a noble-sounding word. It comes from the verb *commit*, a word that always involves *energy* and *time* and *sacrifice*. We all know this. Why do so many of us think we can pour all our best energies into work and church and other projects and still have a happy marriage?

Zack and I have learned we cannot take our marriage or each other for granted. We've learned that the good times, the times of oneness and intimacy, are worth whatever effort is required.

We have been helped by Christian marriage enrichment retreats. We have grown together from good books on marriage. But, most of all, we have talked and talked and talked—gradually learning to admit our needs honestly, to share our dreams, to *accept and affirm* the other. We've learned how to ask specifically for what we want, even if it's as simple as "Would you help me with the dishes tonight?" or as needy as "I just want to know that you appreciate me," rather than pouting because the other didn't read our mind! Asking for what we want doesn't always mean getting what we want, but it opens the door to negotiation and compromise. I'm learning to tell him when he does something that especially pleases me. (Such as, "I like it when you hold hands with me while we're strolling through the mall.") Gradually, we have learned how to *be real with each other.*

There have been a few stretches of painful times when we have shut each other out, become preoccupied with other things, hurt each other through neglect and/or sharp words. Bad times occur in every marriage. I've learned, however, that things can look awfully grim late at night and then look much better when the sun comes up. Bedtime, as everyone tells us, is not the time for confrontation! In our case, the bad times come when we get *too busy, when we allow other interests to rob us of precious time alone with each other.* Facing the problems honestly and giving ourselves the gift of time together restore oneness.

Have I ever thought of divorce? Yes. But never more

than fleetingly. And, happily, not in a long, long time. I mention it only because I suspect many other Christian women, including ministers' wives, may occasionally entertain the thought. If divorce begins to enter your mind as an option, look at it realistically as well as theologically.

In the cases I've known, the one who initiates the divorce usually just exchanges one set of problems for another. Divorce, as I've observed, is usually ugly, always sad, always devastating. I am not judging those who have experienced that heartache. I know from close family ties, one can do everything possible to avoid divorce and it can happen anyway. Human beings make mistakes. There is no question God forgives and restores and gives new life. I serve a God who is in the business of redeeming lives. It is not the purpose of this chapter to deal in depth with divorce. I only want to say, it is dangerous to flirt with the thought of divorce. In a recent study of divorced couples, only 10 percent of those divorced said they had succeeded in improving their lives. If you are at the stage of "just beginning to think about divorce," run, do not walk, to get professional help. It will more than be worth the effort if you can salvage an unhealthy relationship.

For the best marriage, both partners must be willing to accept responsibility for the growth of the marriage. If your mate refuses to admit a need for help, *you* can still seek counseling. You can take the initiative. There are good, Christian therapists who can help you begin to assume more responsibility for your happiness. Happiness really is a choice! When I first heard that statement, it made me angry. I thought, *whoever said that hasn't experienced all that I've experienced. Sometimes we are trapped and can't change the circumstances of our lives.*

Gradually, I've discovered: we can't always change the circumstances of our lives, but we can choose how we respond to those circumstances. We don't have to choose to remain unhappy!

I'm so glad Zack and I continued to hang in there during the tough times! The good times have far outnumbered the unhappy. And, our present stage of life, The Empty Nest, has turned out to be the best yet. Being married to a grandfather is *all right!*

Through these thirty-five years, God has taught us much about real love. He has taught us love is not just an emotion. Our emotions are fickle and absolutely cannot be trusted—especially when we are exhausted or sick or when it has been raining a week! Love is trust, companionship, working together, going to some things together we don't want to attend, learning to fight fair without attacking each other, playing together, forgiving.

I *think* Zack has forgiven me for my faux pas at a Christmas banquet, the annual Deacon-Staff Christmas Banquet at Muskogee. That unforgettable night the banquet program chairman had the idea of asking staff members and their mates to stand and briefly tell about the greatest, most special Christmas they had ever experienced. I spoke just ahead of Zack, and had no trouble instantly remembering the Christmas that stood out in my mind above all others. "The greatest Christmas for me," I announced with a happy smile, "was the Christmas I was ten years old when I received my first horse."

Zack stood and was curiously silent for a long moment. With a funny look on his face, he said, "I guess I know now how I rank—slightly lower than a horse. What none of you know is that it was a Christmas when I asked Nancy to marry me and gave her an engagement ring."

I've had to forgive a few things, too.

Zack has always loved carrot cake and continually asked why I never baked one for him. I didn't want to admit it, but the main reason was that I hated to scrape and grate carrots. One afternoon, feeling sorry for my overworked husband who had to attend a lengthy meeting that night, I decided to make that carrot cake. I was tired after a full day at school, but his joy when I surprised him with the cake would be so rewarding. How pleased he would be to come home and smell the aroma of fresh-baked cake and sit down to unwind with some cake and coffee. I made a special trip to the grocery to buy the ingredients. The finished cake was beautiful. About ten o'clock he arrived home, and I proudly led him to the kitchen where the three-layered cake waited.

"Look!" I beamed. "Look what I made for you! And you'll never guess what kind it is. It's still warm, and I've got coffee brewing."

"Oh, Hon," he said, "I couldn't eat a bite. I'm so full. Our meeting tonight was at the Hales, and Anita served us huge slices of the best carrot cake I've ever eaten."

I've forgiven him. I've just never made another carrot cake.

There have been many compromises. And, there are some things about which we've *never agreed*. That's OK, too. Zack will never understand why I treat a dog like a family member. I will never understand why he insists on keeping and riding a motorcycle! Zack would never have allowed one of our children to have a motorcycle. In fact, we bought our son a horse to get his mind off motorcycles! Yet, after our children were grown, Zack came home one day with a motorcycle. When I accused him of having a mid-life crisis, a friend said, "Count your blessings. Better that he experience his mid-life crisis with a motorcycle than with another woman!

Of course, there is no simple formula for a happy marriage. If there were, we would see more happy marriages. If I summarized the guidelines most helpful to us, I would say: Pray together and pray *for* each other. Be mutually submissive. Keep talking and listening to each other. Play together—often and sometimes impulsively, and whatever it takes to improve your marriage, do it!

The following mini-poster has hung in our bedroom for years:

The Art of Marriage
A good marriage must be created.
In marriage the little things are the big
    things. . . .

It is never being too old to hold hands.
It is remembering to say "I love you" at
    least once a day.

It is never going to sleep angry.
It is having a mutual sense of values and
    common objectives.

It is standing together facing the world.
It is forming a circle of love that gathers
    in the whole family.

It is speaking words of appreciation and
    demonstrating gratitude
    in thoughtful ways.

It is having the capacity to forgive and forget.
It is giving each other an atmosphere
    in which each can grow.

It is a common search for the good and the beautiful.

It is not only marrying the right person—
it is being the right partner.[6]

Lord, thank You for Zack. Thank You for the gift of marriage. Thank you that most of our marriage really has been a GOOD TIME! Help me be the right partner. Teach us both to cherish every day of life together. And, Lord, help Zack to be nicer when the dogs dig in the flower beds. I'll even start riding with him on his motorcycle!

4

His Lovely Wife (Or, Who Am I, Really?)

It was always the same, I thought as I listened to Zack's introduction at the local civic club. Whether we were being introduced to a new church, at a gathering where Zack was to speak, or to whomever, invariably it was, "This is Zack Pannell and his lovely wife."

Have you noticed that ministers' wives are eternally introduced as "the lovely wife of So-and-So"? We are always lovely and we never have any identity of our own!

Recently I was the guest speaker at a banquet where Zack was present. The master of ceremonies (having known me well for years) introduced us (with a twinkle in his eye): "We are delighted tonight to have with us Nancy Pannell and her lovely husband." It made my day!

One's quest for self-discovery is never easy. It is even harder when your identity is inexorably linked with your mate's, and people don't understand his calling and profession.

Even though my husband is an ordained minister (he can marry you, bury you, etc.), he is not a pastor. He is a Minister of Religious Education, which can be kind of hard to explain to non-Baptists. Even some Baptists have a difficult time figuring out exactly what he does besides make announcements on Sunday morning, plan committee meetings, and make them feel guilty for not working in Vacation Bible School.

When introduced to people and asked about my husband's line of work, I say, "He's a Minister of Religious Education." And then they ask, "But what does he do for a living?"

Once, after we'd moved into a new neighborhood and lived there several weeks, we met our neighbors across the street. Inevitably, they asked Zack the question, "And what do you do?" Upon hearing his reply, they remarked, "How interesting. We've noticed you leave the house every morning just like you had a regular job."

Such comments can bring on an identity crisis!

Whether or not people fully comprehend the role of each church staff person, they seem to have very clear notions of what the *staff wife* should be and do! And people in the church are prone to perceive the staff wife only as an extension of her husband. As one book, *The Minister's Mate—Two for the Price of One?*, has already so unequivocally put it, most church members think of the staff wife as an unpaid staff person.

Ancient philosophers pondered the question: "Who am I?" Staff wives still grapple with the same question. It is often pointed out we staff wives wear many hats, as do our husbands. We are expected to be consummate homemakers, wise counselors, competent teachers, gracious hostesses, capable leaders, willing workers, good neighbors, trustworthy friends. In the confusion of all these overlapping, demanding roles, how do we discover our "real selves"?

You are normal if you have wrestled with the question, "Am I called to be what others expect me to be, or am I called to be what God has created in me?" The struggle between these two questions has been the major cause of anxiety in my adult life. All books for ministers' wives encourage us to know ourselves and to be ourselves. Few tell us how to do that. *Knowing ourselves and being ourselves are probably the most difficult things in the world to accomplish!*

About eight years ago I realized Nancy Pannell had gotten lost in the church, her family, and her job. Actually, this chapter is about my personal search for self. I am not so naive as to think it is possible to deal adequately in one chapter or even in one book with the mystery of self-knowledge. It is my hope I can help us *begin* to understand what we mean by "real self," seek out our real selves, and recognize when we are shaping our lives to meet the expectations of others.

It helped me to realize there really is no fixed "real self" inside any of us. John Powell, in his wonderful little book *Why Am I Afraid to Tell You Who I Am?*, reminds us we are all constantly changing. Who we were last year or last week is not the same person we are today. He says, "It is socially fashionable to ask: who are I? There is no little 'real self' inside of me. I am what I am committed to."

He goes on to say, "If I am anything as a person, it is what I think, judge, feel, value, honor, esteem, love, hate, fear, desire, hope for, believe in, and am committed to."[2]

I accept his premise that I can't look inside and find some little person and say, "Oh! There's the real me!" Yet even though I am a life in process, there is a sense in which I can come to know my real identity. To the extent that I can determine what I value...what I believe in...and what I'm committed to, I can determine who I am.

But what's the big deal about knowing self? Why is it

even important to answer: Who am I, really? Why can't we just get on with life and quit being so introspective? Dr. Robert Schuller answers my question with his statement, "Everything we do and are will be a reflection of our self-image, positive or negative."[3] He insists the basic problem in the world today is "many human beings don't realize who they are. And if we don't know who we are and where we have come from, we will never become what we were meant to be."[4]

It is imperative that the staff wife determine *who* she is or she may spend her life trying to be someone else. And that would be a tragedy.

I suggest the first step in finding self is *to determine who or what you are committed to.*

This is likely to be a painful process. Accepting Powell's definition of "real self," I was forced to look deeply within to seek who or what was of major importance to me. How I wanted to say, "I am committed first to God." That's what I had been taught to say. I tried to say, "Lord, you know I love you more than anything or anyone else." But I couldn't.

When we throw away our pretenses and get real with the Lord, He shows us disturbing truth about ourselves.

What a jolt when He revealed that other than my commitment to family, most of my adult life had been committed to *gaining the approval of others.* Most of my life has been spent doing what I perceived others wanted me to do. In that sense, I realized I had been a phony, lacking the courage to be real.

How quickly and easily many of us say, "I am committed to Jesus Christ." I'm beginning to wonder if we have the foggiest notion of what that means. Perhaps we who are saturated in full-time church work, more than anyone else, need to reexamine constantly our commitments, or first priority. Zack has often admitted it is easy for ministers to become so involved with the mechanics of church administration and programming, they lose sight of *why* they are doing those things. All of us who are heavily involved in church need to be aware we can become so committed to a particular emphasis, we lose sight of *why* we are thus involved. We must ever be on guard against the subtle temptation to become committed to *our role or to the strokes we receive for "doing good."*

The desire for approval is powerful motivation. We all want to be liked and affirmed. I have worked fifteen to eighteen hours a day to make sure I had not left a stone unturned in creating the image of Super Mom, Wonder Wife, and Mrs. Church. You know who Mrs. Church is, don't you? She's the one who is trying to do it all. She never misses a thing related to church and she is at church several times a week doing something if she is physically able to move. She always smiles brightly, though the smile may look a little plastic. She may or may not be a staff wife.

Until recently, I lacked the courage to try to determine what God wanted me to do, then to do it. And all the while I was blaming one specific "other" for causing my stress and unhappiness—the church. The church, that nebulous, invisible "they," loomed large in my mind as the culprit who dictated my life-style and pressured me to conform to a certain image.

But the church was not my problem.

Some staff wives may not want to hear this next conclusion. Regardless of whether or not church congregations (or even husbands) put pressure on us, the church is not the primary cause of our stress or unhappiness. As

Pogo said, "We have met the enemy and it is us." My biggest problem was myself.

A few words are in order, I think, about pressure from church members. Let me hasten to recognize: some staff wives may never feel undue pressure from any quarter in the congregation. Many, seemingly, have never struggled with their roles. Even so, some church members, consciously or unconsciously, make excessive demands and have unrealistic expectations of the church staff and mates. I know of no other profession that puts as much subtle but felt pressure *on the mate* to conform to an expected image. As much pressure as there is on the wife of a public official, she at least is not judged on the basis of her spirituality or on whether or not she sings in the choir!

Do church members have a biblical basis for expecting a certain standard of living from the staff wives? Indeed they do. *But not because they are staff wives!* All Christians are called to a standard of godliness. Whether 1 Timothy 3:11 was written to wives of deacons, to women deacons, or to all Christian women, it certainly is applicable to staff wives. It admonishes us, "Women must likewise be dignified, not malicious gossips, but temperate, faithful in all things."

Undoubtedly, we will face some criticism along the way from church members who have unreasonable expectations. But if we consistently think we have a problem with the church, with "them," chances are the church is not our basic problem.

Why does it take us so long to realize and accept the fact that we, and we alone, are responsible for our happiness and are accountable only to God? The answer is, of course, *we don't really want to assume responsibility for our decisions.* That involves risk, and we are afraid to risk. All of us, in varying degrees, are disabled by fears.

If I risk simply being myself, people may not like me. Powell put it so powerfully when he wrote, quoting a young man, "I am afraid to tell you who I am, because, if I tell you who I am, you may not like who I am, and it's all that I have."[5]

Until recently, I felt I must constantly prove I was a person of worth. Thus I agreed to almost everything asked of me if there was any way possible I could manage it. Whatever the request—joining a group, giving a devotional, singing in choir, teaching an extra weeknight Bible study, attending parties, serving on committees—I did it, whether or not I believed it was the best thing to do at the time. You see, if I refused, I might be rejected or censured.

Not only are we afraid to risk rejection, we tend to confuse "being spiritual" with achieving a certain image as the minister's wife. The very nature of our spouse's work creates the potential for guilt trips if we think we are not "dedicated enough." Also, because we love our husbands, we naturally want to avoid at all costs causing him criticism, even if it means allowing ourselves to get squeezed into unsustainable roles.

Most wives (and husbands, too) have accepted some responsibilities or jobs they didn't really want to take on, just to please or help their mates—some of that falls in the category of "Loving Things We Do for Our Spouse." But to live out our lives being unable to say "No" to almost any task because we're afraid of what people will think is tragic.

I'll never forget a conversation that changed my life. Feeling trapped and depressed after overextending myself at church, I complained to a good friend, "I don't have a choice. If I don't do all these things that people expect me to do—as the proper staff wife—Zack will be criticized. I can't let him down."

Jim looked me squarely in the eye and said, "Nancy, you're not as powerful as you think you are."

His response stunned me. "I'm not sure I know what you mean."

"I mean, you don't have as powerful an influence over Zack's life as you think you do. You aren't going to determine Zack's future in the church. I know Zack. He's a good man, and he's a capable, respected leader. The church didn't call him because of you, although you are loved and respected, too; and Zack's future job security is not going to be determined by you."

Wow! If ever someone needed to hear such straight talk, I did.

One consequence of making choices of service based on the expectations of others is that we become trapped in a role. People continue to expect a certain level of visibility, involvement, and activity. If you have been taking on every possible job, you soon create for yourself an untenable posture to maintain. *If your worth is determined by your ability to please and by what you do (rather than by who you are),* it becomes increasingly more difficult to say no to anything. God had to teach me the same lesson He taught Elijah—namely, He has a few other servants. I don't have to do it all!

Our perception of our role as staff wives has been forming since childhood (if we grew up "in church") by messages we received from adults around us. Not unlikely, we heard our pastor's wife faulted about everything from her absence at something to the kind of dress

she wore. I actually heard a church member speak criti-
cally of her pastor's wife because "she always wears
purple"! As staff wives, we've received messages, both
subtle and distinct, from church members, our mates,
and other staff wives.

By and large, the message we *think* we've received is
that we should be "spiritual role models" *because we are
staff wives*. There are two great dangers with this point of
view. First, as already pointed out, one may live out one's
life vainly trying to please others—a route leading only to
frustration and unhappiness. (I'm reminded of the saying,
"The man who trims himself to please others will soon
whittle himself away.") *Second*, there is the danger that
one may begin to see oneself as deserving to be on a
pedestal, as being "super spiritual"—a route leading to
self-righteousness. We are traveling this route when we
want others to see how much we're doing and sacrificing
"for the Lord." Some call this the Martyr Complex. This
route also leads to competition and jealousy between
staff wives, a problem discussed in chapter 7.

Suppose we do some serious soul-searching and discover our commitments are causing us identity problems.
What's next? How can we find strength and freedom to
be ourselves? How have I?

I'm reluctant to venture further with this self-disclosure.
Not because I fear openness, but because I don't want to
sound preachy or simplistic. I have not arrived at some
great spiritual understanding undiscovered by others! If
anything, what I'm about to say shows only what a slow
learner I've been. How could I have so long missed a
truth I've heard taught all my life?

Incredible as it sounds, we can only begin to find and
be ourselves when we start to turn loose of self! Do not

for one moment think I am saying I have grasped complete understanding and mastery of this principle. But, as I slowly grow in the ability to quit focusing on self, I gain strength and freedom to be simply me.

Therefore, I submit the next major step in finding self is *turn loose of self and give all of the self you are aware of to Jesus Christ.*

Recognizing my first commitment had not been to Christ, I began the process of turning over to Him every area of my will and life. Talk about a battle! And the battle is still being waged. However, each time I turn loose, I find more strength and freedom!

We can never really know ourselves until we know Christ. Because He knows and understands every facet of us, only He can give us true self-knowledge. Here's the most exciting part—He doesn't want any of us to be someone else. He made us every one uniquely and wonderfully different. He gives us the freedom to be a one-and-only creation.

Many of us know Christ in a personal relationship, but we still haven't recognized *who we are.* I was taught early the importance of a name. My maiden name was Roberts, and in the Texas community where I grew up, the Roberts's name had stood for integrity and high moral principles for generations. Pride in the family name was instilled in me. When I was growing up, I remember leaving the house and hearing Dad say, "Remember who you are." As a high school student, I remember going on out-of-town, school-sponsored trips and hearing the faculty sponsor say, "Remember who you are. You are representatives of Hamilton High School and your hometown."

Who are we? Just children of God! Just special,

unicue, gifted, loved children of God. I don't have to prove my worth by what I do. My worth is a gift from my Father, the King!

There is a sense in which it may be hard to *accept* who we really are! For so long, I've wanted to be someone else or exactly like someone else. As a teenager, I wanted to be like Babe Didrikson Zaharias, to me the greatest woman athlete in history. As an adult, I've wanted to be as witty a speaker as Jeannette Clift George, as good a writer as Catherine Marshall, as wise or as spiritually discerning as all those whose lives (or words) have influenced me. It can be tough to come to terms with *who we are not*, as well as with *who we are*. But it's liberating and fun to keep discovering one's real self.

We can have the right theology and still find it almost impossible to lose ourselves in complete abandonment to Him. This surrendering all of self has been the most difficult thing for me in the Christian walk. I seem to have an enormous self-will. Yet, whenever I succeed in turning loose of self (at least, as much of self as I'm aware of), I not only find strength to *be*, I find freedom from fear of what others will think. Christ wants us to be free of fears, free of the burden of trying to prove our worth, free of self-pity, free of anxiety brought on by being too stressed-out. Surrender to Christ brings freedom. As others have already discovered and pointed out, a great paradox of the Christian life is that in turning loose of self, we are set free. We find Jesus telling us in Matthew 16:25, "but whoever loses his life for My sake *shall find it*" (author's italics).

Another thing about surrender of self and total commitment: it is not something I can do once and then be ever after totally surrendered! It is something I must do daily, even many times daily! But everytime I surrender my will, my anxieties, my resentments, I find freedom and strength and peace.

The next step in finding self is *spend time alone with the Master, letting Him impress you with what He would have you do, with whom He would have you become.*

He will likely begin to show you actions and attitudes you need to put out of your life, as well as those you need to take on. I'm trying to learn to take every decision to Him and seek His guidance. Sometimes His directions are clear, sometimes more difficult to discern. He has not sent me any visions! He makes impressions upon me through His Word, through His Spirit within me, and through others.

Here's the neat part: *He is teaching me I really can choose to do only what He impresses me to do.* When I am following His guidance, I don't feel a need to explain and justify my decisions. His loving Spirit affirms me and is constantly teaching me to accept myself and feel good about myself. Along with self-acceptance, He is also teaching me to *accept others*—even if they disagree with me! It's been very liberating to realize that others don't have to agree with me or share my values. The opinions of others do not determine my worth.

A great way to spend time alone with the Lord is through Christian meditation, a discipline I'm only beginning to learn and practice. Christian meditation is focusing on the Presence of the Lord and listening to Him. Generally, when we approach God, we tend to do all the talking. It's not easy to quiet our minds and concentrate on His Presence. Though still a novice in meditation, Christ has given me direction when I've gone to Him meditatively, willing to listen, and receive guidance.

Dr. Richard Foster has written enlightening and challenging ideas on the discipline of meditation. He explains, "Christian meditation leads us to the inner wholeness necessary to give ourselves to God freely. . . . Often meditation will yield insights that are deeply practical, almost mundane."[6]

I particularly liked his thoughts about the practical benefits of meditation. Through meditation, Christ has impressed upon me specific actions I needed to take. He has given me insights regarding people I needed to pray for, encouragement I needed to give, notes I needed to write, people I needed to forgive.

Realistically, I recognize it is almost impossible for the woman who has children at home, who is working outside the home, to find time for meditation. It requires great effort just to find time for personal Bible study. Surely, it's unrealistic to think the typical young wife and mother can find additional time for meditation. Let me urge you to be alert to those little moments when you can retreat from the frantic pace of the day and listen to the Lord. such as moments when the children are down for a nap, during your lunch break at work, before the family has awakened. We are all quite exercise-conscious these days. I've found an excellent time to listen to the Lord is while walking.

Logically, the next step in finding self is *dare to be obedient to His leading.*

That's another way of saying, dare to risk. As He gives insight, we must dare to follow His prodding. You may ask, "What if I risk being truly myself as He reveals and I get shot down and wounded?" Getting wounded is a strong possibility! Stepping out in obedience, of course, involves trust. We have to believe He will enable us to be and do whatever He has impressed us to be and do. *And we have to trust Him with the consequences when we are being obedient.* My friend and former pastor, Dr. Warren Hultgren, said in a sermon, "As difficult as it is to live His way, it is far more difficult not to live His way."

Blindly following Him is scary! But it can be exciting, too. That is the heart of chapter 6.

Admittedly, surrendering all of self to Christ is the most difficult thing in the world for me. Obviously, the reason it is so hard to surrender and obey is because I have difficulty trusting Him! Oh, it's easy to trust God to save my soul. It's easy to trust Him to take care of me throughout eternity. It's even fairly easy for me to trust Him to provide for my material needs. The tough part is trusting Him with the details of my everyday life! You see, He might require something of me I'm afraid to do. He might want me to give up something I enjoy doing, confess something locked inside, forgive someone I don't want to forgive, share my faith.

My capacity to trust was significantly increased one March morning in 1982. I had just come through a long ordeal of flu when a doctor discovered a blood clot in my leg and confined me to bed. I was not only a little anxious about myself, I was also floundering in a sea of personal problems. I was having relationship problems with a colleague at work and feeling like a miserable failure as a mother and as a wife—particularly as the wife of a minister. Lying with my leg propped up, I had considerable time to read again the Gospel of John and got only as far as these words: "He created everything there is—nothing exists that he didn't make" (1:3, TLB).

The thought leaped out at me: If He has the power and wisdom to create all things, surely He is powerful and wise enough for me to trust Him with every detail of my life. Surely I can trust Him with my relationships and with the consequences of being obedient to Him.

The rest of the morning I did a search of all the Scriptures I could find on trust. From Psalm 56 I read, "But when I am afraid, I will put my confidence in you. Yes, I will trust the promises of God" (v. 3, TLB).

The psalmist continues, "And since I am trusting him, what can mere man do to me?" (v. 4, TLB).

In Psalm 33 I found, "No wonder we are happy in the Lord! For we are trusting him. We trust his holy name" (v. 21, TLB).

Funny, how verses we've heard all our lives suddenly take on new meaning. I became convinced that day that we are really happy only when we trust Him. I recovered from more than just a blood clot; I recovered from a doubt clot. Not that doubts haven't resurfaced, but I've been better able to deal with them.

Here is a very simple illustration of the practical application of trust. If I believe He has called me to teach a particular Sunday School class, I must trust Him to enable me to do it. If I believe He wants me *not* to teach that class at this time, I must trust Him to give me peace of mind about my decision. On a deeper level, if I believe He has called me to take an unpopular stand or even to radically change my life, I must trust Him with the consequences He may call me to follow Him to a foreign mission field or to sacrifice personal ambition for my mate. He calls all of us to confront injustice and prejudice wherever we find it, and it is all around us, even at church.

The last step in finding self is *recognize the process of self-discovery is ongoing, never ending.*

Just as we never arrive at spiritual perfection, we never arrive at complete understanding of self, since self is constantly in a state of transition. I'm glad the real me is changing!

I hope I am more compassionate, more loving, more tolerant and forgiving than I was ten years ago—than I was yesterday. Yesterday I learned that a young friend is suffering tragically from dependence on drugs. As we visited together and I shared in the pain, I changed some more. I grasped more fully how vulnerable and fragile we *all* are.

The more self-understanding we gain, the easier it becomes to recognize when we are doing good things for the wrong reasons. *We can be pretty sure we are shaping our lives to meet the expectations of others if we've lost all joy in service.* If we continue on that course, whether staff wife or layperson, we can expect to become depressed or physically ill or both. Powell also wrote, "When I repress my emotions, my stomach keeps score."[7] Many staff wives are chronically ill. The illnesses are real, but I wonder how many of them are brought on because of repressed resentments or fears.

Some staff wives rebel by trying to shock. They may wear radically different clothes or try to shock by their speech. I've had a bent in that direction, but lacked the courage to be too outrageous! If, however, one sees oneself having a perverse desire to shock, let me pass on a thought that has helped me. Our need to shock is probably a deep need to be loved, accepted, and understood. The more I grasp and accept Christ's unconditional love, the less I feel a need to be aggressively and shockingly different!

Acknowledging we all need positive strokes and we all

need to serve, how do we go about "finding our niche" and "doing our thing"? Let me suggest something so simple and practical. Think about what you enjoy and do well. You may call it your strong point or skill (chances are, it's a spiritual gift), but zero in on it. Focus on one main thing, rather than fragmenting yourself in many directions. Concentrate on developing one primary interest. It may be in the realm of music or teaching or organizing or ministering to others—but focus on one area. That is, unless you really are Superwoman!

Jesus gives each of us permission to be our own person, to be real. That's exciting! Understand, I haven't arrived in self-understanding and self-assurance! I still catch myself jockeying for "Staff Wife of the Year" and have to rein in and ask, "Nance, are you going like gangbusters to make sure everyone thinks you're wonderful, or are you being led by the Spirit?"

I wish I could erase from the minds of all ministers' wives their stereotyped ideas of the model minister's wife. We do not have to be a combination of wonderful, sweet, efficient Mary Poppins, ambitious Mrs. Church, and Joan of Arc, martyr extraordinaire. How much healthier, both spiritually and physically, we would be if we could simply *be whoever we are* and let God direct our choices. I have tasted the liberation that comes from being authentic rather than shaping my life to meet the expectations of others. God never overburdens me.

I wrote this chapter before coming across these words of Elizabeth McBurney:

> The real you is precious and unique and will be a gift to everyone around you. It will be a wonderful gift to you to be free of the bondage of trying to be someone else. I wouldn't trade that freedom for millions of dollars. I can

attest that life being the real me is great. People are wonderful as they respond to truth rather than phoniness, and I am free to be more loving and giving than I ever was in bondage. Of course, this does not eliminate all problems from my life, but they affect me differently, and I respond to them in a different way.[8]

Who am I? I am a child of God who wears many hats. But not as many as I used to try to wear! God is continuing to show me the ones He wants me to wear.

At the age of fifty-five, I finally can say that the hat I enjoy wearing most bears the caption *His Child*. Next is the one labeled *Wife*. I'm grateful I am still able to put on the hat bearing the label *Daughter*. How joyful it is to put on the hats identified as *Mother, Grandmother, Sister*. Apart from family, I love the hats called *Friend, Teacher,* and *Colaborer*.

Dear Lord, keep calling me back to You when my commitment strays. Show me when I'm puffed up with pride and self-righteousness. Show me when I'm striving just to impress others. Lord, I know I'm still a mess, but You've given me permission not only to BE me, but to LIKE me. What a wonderful feeling! Thank You!

5 Dragons on the Doorstep

"I didn't even know we had any dragons in our church," said M., a pastor's wife and close friend, "then we came home from the SBC convention to find them camped on our doorstep. Now, they've moved into the garage, and, at the rate they are gathering steam, they'll soon be in the living room."

My friend was not hallucinating nor had she gone completely around the bend. Having read Marshall Shelley's *Well-Intentioned Dragons (Ministering to Problem People in the Church)*, I knew exactly what she meant. All of us in ministry have met a few dragons—some well-intentioned and some whose intentions were highly suspect. According to Shelley, dragons in the church are "often sincere, well-meaning saints, but they leave ulcers, strained relationships, and hard feelings in their wake . . . for some reason, they undermine the ministry of the church."[1] Dragons in the church may attack any church member, but their prime targets are staff and families. Some attack subtly with inferences that cast doubt; some attack openly, directly. Some dragons only irritate like a pebble in the shoe. Some are as destructive as a U.S. Patriot missile!

M. sat across from me in the little secluded restaurant

where we often met to bare our souls, cry occasionally, and laugh a lot. Her call that morning from a nearby city simply said, "Help! I need a dragon slayer. Can we meet for lunch?" By the sparkle in her eye and her quick chuckle, I knew the dragons had not defeated her. She was a little singed by their fiery breathings, but her sense of humor was intact.

It's always a shock to discover somebody actually doesn't love us! Especially since we're so lovable! Disagree with us? Sure. Misunderstand us? Sure. But not love us? Unbelievable!

Let me underscore: Most congregations are supportive of their staffs and their families. The greatest blessings to Zack and me have been the gifts of love and friendship throughout our ministry from people of all ages and all walks of life. We've received far more than we've given. Yet, the reality for families in the ministry is that the minister's family always has been and probably always will be carefully scrutinized and criticized by some in the church family. Some church members have been known to keep a record of your every activity—including how many times you miss church and, incredible as it sounds, how much money you are giving! The good news is, that attitude is not characteristic of most church members. Nevertheless, as is true for all people with high public profiles,

- not everyone will love you,
- not everyone will understand you,
- not everyone will agree with you, and
- some will be quick to criticize, slow to affirm.

This reality goes with the turf. The best advice one can give or receive is deal with it. We *can* deal with it, even when the dragons move into the living room.

It seems the dragons come at us when we least expect them. I can recall confiding to a friend, "Just when I think things are going well, when I'm feeling good about life in general, someone blindsides me with something about which I'm totally innocent! For instance, I'll be told that Mrs. So-and-So is offended because I didn't speak to her—and I didn't even know I'd been near her."

My staff-wife friend nodded sympathetically. "I know what you mean. I just found out a family was very angry with my husband and me because we didn't visit them while the husband was in the hospital. We didn't know he was in the hospital. No one had called the church or our home to report it."

Through the last thirty-five years, word has come back to me of all manner of criticisms of my husband, of me, and, occasionally, of our children. Some were justified, most were petty (some even made us laugh), but others made deep wounds. I've come to understand the following words of the military psychiatrist on television's "MASH": "It's the little battlefields that leave the worst scars."

The possibility always exists that dragons have a valid reason for righteous indignation. Such as the time a horde of angry women descended upon Zack the first day of Vacation Bible School. The "old-timers" at First Baptist, Muskogee, will still tell you about the time their Minister of Education was almost fired over doughnuts. They laugh about it now. They weren't laughing that day twenty-five years ago! Zack has always been a conservative spender. (He calls it *conservative*; I have another word for it.) While planning for the summer Vacation Bible School that year, he examined the budgets of past Vacation Bible Schools and decided a major expenditure could be cut. The church had, for as far back as anyone could remember, provided coffee and doughnuts for the volunteer adult workers for their break times. Without consulting anyone, he made an high-level executive decision. He would provide doughnuts and coffee, but charge the workers for their refreshments. On the first day of Vacation Bible School, the refreshment table bore a sign announcing the cost of purchasing the desired refreshments. Consumers were placed on an honor system—they could leave money in a cup beside the sign.

Opening days of Vacation Bible School, like first days of any school, are hectic at best. This day was memorable. The first group of workers to see the sign and cup spread the word. Within moments, the women were outside Zack's office, and they were not happy campers.

I wasn't there, so I can't really say what happened, but it was reported to me that phrases like "We can't *believe* you would charge volunteer workers who are sacrificing their time, . . ." and "This church has *always*, . . ." and "If we're *that* short of funds, maybe we need to cut some salaries." As in *The Duel* by Eugene Field, "The air was littered, an hour or so,/With bits of gingham and calico." Unlike the gingham dog and the calico cat, they didn't eat each other up. They reached a solution. The offending sign and cup disappeared and free doughnuts and coffee were back the next day. No salaries were cut. Sometimes, a graceful retreat with an admission of error is the wisest course.

A few times (well, maybe more than a few) I've given church members cause for ire. Church members surely have the right to expect their staff wives to behave with decorum at church. Most of the time I do. (Why, I've pondered, do things seem funnier during a solemn church service?)

The man sitting in the pew in front of me was a new Christian. He was one of the most transformed, sincere, zealous Christians I'd ever met. We all loved him and rejoiced in his transformation, but he was almost too much. His boundless energy and endless new ideas for church evangelistic projects soon exhausted all who worked with him. He wanted to evangelize the world in one day. And when he was called on to pray, he prayed and prayed and prayed. He talked rapidly and about every third or fourth word he readdressed God. That particular Sunday he was asked to pray. "Oh, Father," he began, then quickly, "God, we just want to say, Father, how much we, God, thank You for today, and, Father, You know that, God, we just. . . ."

I was sitting beside one of our staff wives, which was a mistake, because she was as irreverent as I. The longer his prayer stretched and the more "Fathers" and "Gods" he injected, the more LaVon and I began to shake. I elbowed her, meaning, "Cool it, or I'll lose it."

But then, the inevitable happened. As his "Fathers" and "Gods" got closer together, with rising voice he implored, "And, oh *Fod*. . . ."

She and I both lost it. We strangled trying to choke back our laughter. We doubled over in the pew, holding our hands over our mouths, shaking and laughing. I don't know when he stopped praying or anything else that happened that morning. The demon of hilarity consumed us, and, every few minutes throughout the rest of the service one of us would tremble with suppressed giggles. Everytime I thought of "Fod" it took all my concentration to keep from bursting into peals of laughter.

No disciplinary committee called upon us, but as I was leaving church, one dignified lady made a noise that sounded like a "Hhhmph," or something similar. And I thought I heard her say, "If children behaved that way...." Maybe we avoided big-time trouble because LaVon and I quit sitting together for awhile.

Occasionally I've had the eerie feeling that my personal life was being telecast over a giant video screen with all the church invited to view! I was attending a bridal shower several years ago for a young woman in our church. An impressive crowd was present, and I floated from one group to another, enjoying the fellowship. One woman, who had been quite active in our church at one time and whose husband had served on several key church committees, turned to me.

"I hear you are thinking of retiring from teaching," she noted.

"Yes!" I affirmed enthusiastically, "At last! I can hardly wait. After twenty-five years of working full time, I've got lots of plans for my post-teaching days. One of the things I'm looking forward to is having time to go to lunch with friends." Then I jokingly added, "Of course, after I quit work, I may not be able to afford to go out to lunch very often!"

She looked at me without a hint of a smile and said, "Oh, my Dear, you'll be able to afford it. We know exactly what your husband earns."

Her words jolted me, but not as much as my first experience of sitting in a church business meeting and listening, mortified, while my husband's salary was discussed and debated, along with his worth. Since that horrendous night I've generally made it a practice to be absent from church business meetings when the budget is discussed. Of course, my husband can't be absent. Admittedly, church members provide the money and have the right to know what the salaries are. But there are ways, now adopted by many churches, of handling this matter with sensitivity. Many churches have a budget committee prepare and present for their consideration a budget which lumps all salaries in one category; then if members wish to know the breakdown of individual salaries, they can request and receive that information privately.

Not all verbal assaults are small matters. Sometimes they pierce to the core, particularly when they hurt our children. At a sister church, the pastor was under fire. In a called business meeting, a few deacons roasted him mercilessly while his wife and teenage daughter sat in stunned disbelief. Unfounded charges were made that he had used church money for his own personal affairs and that he had lied. His wife left soon after the meeting started, taking their daughter with her, but it was too late to prevent the trauma. With tears streaming down her face, the daughter cried, "Why would they say those things about Daddy? He has never done a dishonest thing in his life." The charges were later proven to be totally false, but the scars on the family will last forever.

The only thing fathers and mothers can do at these times is provide such a bulwark of love within the family circle that children feel secure in spite of flames from the dragons. Children should be encouraged to talk about their feelings, but parents should refrain from excessive talking about church problems in front of their children.

A staff wife wrote to me, "The hardest thing I have to live with is harsh and unfair criticism of my husband. I know he isn't perfect, but I know his heart. I know he loves the Lord and is striving to please Him. It hurts so much to see him attacked. How can I handle this?"

I understand. I feel the pain in her heart. I've experienced the same pain and voiced the same words.

There are some positive and biblical ways we can deal with the dragons. First, we need to take inventory and make sure we are not just being paranoid, just creating imaginary dragons due to our own low self-esteem. Some people see dragons lurking behind every door. If, in truth, someone's negative spirit is causing us considerable stress, we might ask: Would the situation best be handled by going to that person in loving confrontation or would it be best just to evaluate the criticism objectively, accept it if it is valid, then get on with other things?

If someone is attacking you and spreading untruths or if someone is angry or offended by something you've done (or that they *think* you've done), go to that person in love. *Listen* with an open ear, an open mind, and an open heart. I've often seen my gracious husband completely disarm an angry church member by simply listening to all the person had to say, giving him or her an opportunity to vent feelings. Pray with the person. Often, this biblical way of dealing with problem relationships solves the problem.

On the other hand, people may reject our attempts at reconciliation. "We've called them and written them notes asking if they will let us come by to talk. They won't respond," said M. "We don't know anything else to do, but continue to pray."

I reaffirmed what she already knew. When you've done all you can do to restore broken fellowship, then square your shoulders, hold your head high, keep on serving the Lord, and trust Him. He can be trusted to bring us through the fire. He understands. There were dragons in Jerusalem two thousand years ago.

Sometimes we don't even know who the dragon is!

The anonymous letter cut to the quick. Its bitter attack of my husband hurt more than anything I'd ever experienced. It was unfair, as are all anonymous letters. I was home alone when the letter arrived, and for awhile I wept. Then the self-pity turned to anger I engaged in several heated mental discussions. I fantasized about reading the letter in front of the whole church (and, of course, eliciting much sympathy and embarrassing the writer). For several days I brooded and fed my resentment and was general disgruntled.

But one morning, weary of carrying the heavy burden of hurt and anger, I decided to give the letter and its writer to the Lord.

"Well, here they are," I said to Him, feeling more than a bit self-righteous for doing what I'd known all along I needed to do. "You deal with it in Your way."

It wasn't to be quite that simple.

You need to pray for the letter writer, He seemed to say.

"I don't want to pray for him or her. I feel more like telling him or her where to go, if I just knew who—whom—to go after."

You need to pray for this person. And you need to forgive.

I didn't want to forgive. I've always identified with Jeannette Clift George who reported this internal argument with God: "Lord, I'm going to give it to You straight. I really feel I can't forgive them. Because, in the first place, You're going to forgive them, and if one of us doesn't hold on, they'll get off scot-free!"

God wouldn't let it lie. I knew Him well enough to know He would be just like my granddaughters when they wanted my attention. He would keep tugging at my sleeve until I yielded to Him. Reluctantly, I began to pray for that one who obviously was burdened with much anger. Not surprisingly, as I continued to pray, God gave me complete peace.

We, like many families of ministers, have faced assaults by the dragons that stunned and bewildered, the betrayal of people we thought were close friends, false accusations. At times we've wanted to run away from it all. My next words are going to sound like the cliché "Just pray about it," but there's really only one way to handle this kind of hurt. Give it totally to the Lord. You're right, it's not easy. Giving it to the Lord means: Quit brooding over it, *quit talking about it, particularly to people in the church.* Let go of your hurt and let Him fight your battles for you. You *can* and He *will!*

From *The Living Bible* we read: "Give your burdens to the Lord. He will carry them. He will not permit the godly to slip or fall" (Ps. 55:22).

Interestingly, the more comfortable and accepting I become with myself, the better able I am to evaluate painful criticism without letting it "eat my lunch." But don't think I've arrived at the point where I always immediately practice what I'm preaching.

Church members with a critical spirit can make our lives royally miserable, if we *choose* to let them. Ah, that's the key—making a considered choice. We don't have to choose to let them determine our happiness. That's neither an original nor a pious statement. I'm expressing a truth that took me fifty years to grasp! When we choose to let the dragons make us miserable, they have won, whether we stay in the church or leave.

French novelist George Sand had something to say about how to be happy in spite of trials: "One is happy... once one knows the necessary ingredients of happiness—simple tastes, a certain degree of courage, self-denial to a point, love of work, and, above all, a clear conscience."

A *clear conscience!* That's the secret ingredient. I'm reminded of a conversation with Zack, who has never been as disturbed by dragons as I. "How can you appear so unruffled about this?" I asked him, feeling almost miffed at his casual attitude. "Those were horrible things they said about you and they're not true." (It simply wasn't fair for me to have to do all the worrying.)

"Nance, if you want to stew over it and lie awake at nights, go ahead. I believe I'm where the Lord wants me to be and doing, as best as I can interpret His leadership, what He wants me to do. My conscience is clear. I'm not going to worry about it."

There is an update on my friend M. God has not only seen them through the fire, He has opened up doors to an even better and more exciting opportunity for service! Isn't that just like Him?!

Lord, I acknowledge that You never promised us an easy go of it. But You did promise always to be with us, and You've never broken that promise. Help me to forgive the dragons when my inclination is to slay them. Help me to leave the dragon-fighting to You.

6 Living in the "Real World"

I used to come home from a day at school—from smoke-filled faculty lounges where, believe me, slices of *real* life were aired; from coping with sexually explicit and suicidal notes written by students; from exposure to constant vulgarities in the hallways; from weeping over abused teens and pregnant thirteen-year-olds—and say to Zack, "You're not living in the real world. You're down at the church interacting for the most part with church members, absorbed with your organizations at church. You don't know what it's like out in the real world!"

This is a dilemma for ministers and wives. Not that my life was enhanced by sexually explicit notes and vulgar language, but at least I was confronted by reality in the world and challenged to "be in the world but not of the world." The very nature of our husbands' work causes us to become so engaged with the local church, we develop tunnel vision or become spiritually myopic. Yet the very nature of the work *should* be propelling us out into the world beyond the church, out into the marketplace.

This chapter asks the question, "What are you doing besides going to church?"

If your family is still at home, or you're working outside the home, or *both*, I can just hear your response to that question! It might not be nice! However, the premise of this chapter is that we Christians do a great deal more talking about being salt in the world than we accomplish being salty.

In her book *Out of the Salt Shaker and into the World*, Rebecca Manley Pippert asks how we can be the salt of the earth if we never get out of the salt shaker. She develops these ideas:

- Jesus said we are salt and light.
- We are to make a difference in the world because we are different.
- We can't make a difference in the world if all our time away from home is spent in the salt shaker, our closely-knitted Christian community.[1]

Along with Pippert, I believe we American Christians have become *insulated* and *isolated* from the world we've been told to permeate. Even if you feel like you are already working a thirty-hour day, I'm going to suggest there are ways you can be involved in the world outside your safe, secure group. In other words, this chapter is about some practical ways we can get saltier.

Opportunities are all around us. We can share a part of our lives, in a more than casual way, with those outside our church family. Being alert to opportunities to minister to and befriend people is the way to begin.

Probably the first place to start is in our neighborhood. Too often in the past, some of our nonchurchgoing neighbors were the first to reach out a helping hand or make overtures of friendship. We were too busy going to church.

We've returned from vacation to find our lawn mowed by a considerate neighbor. Once, when I was home alone and accidentally triggered our burglar alarm, three neighbor men appeared at my door almost instantly, armed with baseball bats and bricks! When our beloved dog died one evening while we were away, a neighbor came and put our Sasha's body in a box. He knew how painful it would be for us to handle the lifeless form. A small thing, but a caring thing to do.

Interestingly, none of the neighbors mentioned were churchgoing people. Some of them had life-styles radically different from ours. The gentle neighbor who helped when our pet died, and who on another occasion chased a would-be burglar from our front yard, lived down the street with a woman who was not his wife.

You may ask, "What's your point?" My point is, those outside our Christian community often put us to shame for our glaring lack of involvement with people other than "our own kind." Those neighbors, who did not think of themselves as religious persons, taught me about being Christian. They cared about us and were willing to get involved.

Do you have any idea who's hurting or celebrating in your neighborhood? Do you know the names of your neighbors? Do you ever spend time simply visiting with them *as a friend*—not as "the minister's wife"? Have you ever considered having a backyard neighborhood cookout or inviting neighbors over for a holiday open house? We can begin being salt in our own neighborhoods.

Many Christians are also so nearsighted they scarcely know other believers outside their persuasion exist. We tend to suffer from exclusivism, feeling very threatened when we move outside our little sphere of "like faith." Have you cultivated friends outside your religious affiliation? It's OK, you know, for Protestants to have Catholic or Jewish friends! My across-the-street, Catholic neighbor in Tulsa was one of my prayer partners. I suspect her prayers had a great deal to do with the selling of our home when the time came for us to move. Does your town or city have a ministerial wives' fellowship? If it doesn't, why don't you consider starting one? No telling what might happen if the Baptist and Methodist and Presbyterian and Lutheran and Episcopalian, etc. ministers' wives started getting together! This could be a rich support group, and it could help us overcome anxiety about circulating outside our comfort zone.

Other writers have already proposed many practical ways to get involved in the real world. If you work outside the home, cultivate friends at work. Join a civic club. Work in P.T.A. Keep yourself informed about what's happening in your local and state government and write letters when needed. Vonette Bright in *For Such a Time as This* said, "I encourage Christian women to be involved in at least one secular organization... Christian women do not have to run an organization to exert influence ... God doesn't give the Christian the alternative of feeling bored and unfulfilled."[2]

God has placed in my path many wonderful people outside our church family. He has given me innumerable opportunities to be salt, and most of the time I've blown it by being too dense or too insecure or too busy. But there are two unique personal experiences I want to relate to show how God can enrich our lives *when we take a step beyond the church.*

A friend once said to me, "No one comes into our lives by accident." God may not have orchestrated the meeting between Connie and me, but He surely smiled a lot during our budding friendship. Connie was a colleague with whom I shared a planning period at school. Indisputably, we were hardly candidates for "best friends." Based on her own self-analysis, Connie was an agnostic who had a dim view of most evangelicals.

When we met, Connie was trying to put her life back together after a shattering divorce. She had a pretty grim opinion of the world in general and men in particular. Though she was at times cynical, I quickly discovered Connie was one of the most intelligent, witty, caring, persons I had ever known.

Our friendship soon extended beyond school, even though our life-styles could hardly have been more different. When we met for dinner on some of those nights Zack had meetings at church, Connie drank Scotch while I drank coffee. Her vocabulary was a little more colorful than mine. She occasionally tried to shock me with her skepticism, telling me of all the preachers she'd known who had been unfaithful to their wives or who, according to her perspective, were strictly con artists out to fleece the world. She had worked with far too many church-going colleagues who had been blatantly hypocritical.

In spite of our different philosophies of life, the times we spent together were some of the best times I've ever experienced. She challenged my mind. She understood and sympathized when I was down. Her witty insights made me laugh. I listened and sympathized with her trials of singleness.

Perhaps not to my credit, I was rather pleased the day she introduced me to another of her friends with, "This is my friend, Nancy. You'd never guess she was a minister's wife!"

Several interesting things happened during the evolution of our friendship. I discovered my horizons were being broadened, helping me to break loose of tunnel vision. Connie cut right through religious pretensions and clichés. She could spot a phony in an instant. She made me be real.

Which brings to mind something I've been wanting to say for a long time... we Christians need to retire our in-house, church vocabulary and begin to talk real if we want the rest of the world to listen. It's possible to be a Christian and not say "share" or "Praise the Lord."

We go around abounding in "spiritual" words and phrases. Must we always *share* instead of *tell*? Why can't we simply *pray for* instead of *lift up* each other? Why do we *say just* more frequently than athletes say *you know*? Listen to a group of evangelicals in conversation. We seem to want to *just share* everything!

Walter Hooper, former private secretary to C. S. Lewis, in writing a study guide to *The Screwtape Letters*, suggested we send many overworked words to a Rest Home for Tired Words. He allowed, "Some arrangements could no doubt be made for 'visiting hours,' "[3] but asserted that many vogue words deserved a much-needed rest. The non-Christian world is neither impressed by nor attracted to our religious verbiage. The non-Christian world is looking for authenticity as well as love from professing Christians.

The non-Christian world is looking for acceptance, too. We don't have to change our standards to accept others unconditionally. Regrettably, too many zealously religious people never cultivate a close friendship with someone other than "their own kind."

Not only did Connie teach me much, God taught me a lesson I've never forgotten. During the first year of my growing friendship with Connie, I was too bound by fear of rejection to talk to her about Christ. I tried to live before her in a positive Christian way, but I was literally intimidated by her quick mind. I was afraid she might shred my theology as well as our relationship if I started any Jesus talk.

One summer day she telephoned for a luncheon date. God had been working on me, impressing me with the conviction that it was time to talk to Connie about Him. I had been authentic with her in every way but one. I had never been honest with Connie about what Christ meant to me.

While driving to the restaurant to meet Connie, I wrestled with the Lord. I was so nervous and agitated, I couldn't look forward to our lunch. God was putting me in a bind. There was not a doubt in my mind He wanted me to tell Connie about my relationship to Him, and I was scared.

"Lord," I pleaded, "I don't want to alienate her. I love her."

I love her, too, He seemed to say.

"But, Lord, I'm not clever enough to answer all her arguments. What you're asking may destroy our friendship."

And then, God impressed me with these words as surely as if He had spoken out loud: *Nancy, you can trust me with your friendships.*

I met Connie. We finished our meal, and we lingered, talking about school, our kids. Finally, I could stand it no longer.

"Connie," I blurted out, "I've got to talk to you about something." I don't remember all I said, but I remember saying in conclusion. "I've been a different sort of hypocrite. Instead of pretending to be better than I was, I've pretended to be worse than I was."

Her smile was knowing and affectionate as she said, "You haven't fooled me! I knew all along what you believed!"

What a lesson! God was powerful enough to sustain our friendship, and He was powerful enough to reveal Himself through me in spite of my weakness.

Connie did not indicate that she was buying into my beliefs, but she did listen courteously and attentively. Our friendship continues. Even though I've moved to another city, she and I have kept in touch. I pray for Connie to find her way to our loving God. I believe she will, or perhaps, already has.

God can be trusted with all our relationships.

He can also be trusted to enable us to do whatever He asks us to do. Even is it means bringing a stranger from another culture into our home. Let the record show, following our Lord is never dull!

Being salt and light dramatically rearranged our comfortable lives about five years ago. One fall morning at breakfast, we noted a news article about a student foreign exchange program. Casually, while sipping a second cup of coffee, we discussed the possibility of "someday" taking a student. As Zack left for work, he said, "Why don't you write for information? Just ask them to mail us some brochures and stuff."

The exchange program didn't mail us anything. They telephoned. Would we please consider taking a young Brazilian, seventeen-year-old Eduardo Paes, for the second high school semester?

We had been completely free of the responsibility of parenting for eight years. We loved the freedom and intimacy that had come with the departure of our children. Surely we were crazy even to consider this drastic modification of our lives! Surely there were plenty of mission opportunities all around us. Surely we didn't need to bring a teenager from another land into our home in order to be salt!

God wouldn't leave us alone (that's another of His annoying habits). A few telephone calls and many prayers later, we agreed to take Eduardo as "our son" for five and a half months. It's probably good that we did not know how much our lives would change with his coming!

And now, I want to tell about Eduardo, even though the telling could be a whole book in itself. The best way for his story to be told is through the pages of a journal I kept.

Saturday, 10 January, 1987. I don't know how to begin expressing the excitement, the anticipation, the nervousness and the happiness of this day. For weeks all I've thought about has been *When Eduardo gets here. . . .* Today he arrived! Eduardo da costa Paes from Rio de Janeiro has come to live with us. I'll never forget my excitement this afternoon at the airport when we saw him for the first time. We were holding a big sign saying "WELCOME EDUARDO!" He ran to us, embraced us, and said, "My new mom and dad!" He is such a happy, courteous, friendly, good-looking young man, and he speaks English exceptionally well. Our kids met us for dinner. They, too, have been enthusiastic about his coming. I have the feeling we're starting an awesome adventure, but I feel good about it. I'm sure there will be adjustments for us as well as for Eduardo. One thing I've already learned about him— he loves hamburgers and chocolate chip cookies!

Sunday, 11 January. We left Eduardo sleeping this

morning while we went to church. He had a long journey and was up late unpacking. I don't know if he will choose to attend church with us or not, but, certainly, we won't pressure him about church. When we got home, we found Eduardo very depressed and homesick. Tearfully, he said, "They told us it would be like this, but I didn't expect to feel this bad." We were prepared, too, for cultural shock to hit him, but hadn't expected it quite so soon. We encouraged him to talk about his feelings. We invited some young people from church to drop by this afternoon to meet him. I think he felt a little better by the time they left.

Tuesday, 20 January. Eduardo is still pretty bewildered by high school and life here. Almost everything is radically different from the culture he left. He left a beautiful home on a beach in Rio. Texas in winter is an abrupt change from the beauty of Rio! He is accustomed to many maids. He's also accustomed to a great deal of personal freedom. Our lack of anything alcoholic in the house is incomprehensible to him! Tonight Eduardo introduced me to part of *his* culture. He taught me to cook black beans and rice, Brazilian style. We went to the grocery store together to find all the necessary ingredients—garlic, bay leaves, sausage, pork fat. While it was cooking, he said, "This smells like my mother's kitchen." He was delighted with the black beans and rice but disappointed we had no beer. It seems one is supposed to drink beer with black beans and rice! I tried to explain the Baptist position (though hardly a widespread Baptist practice), but of course he finds it strange. Once when he was feeling particularly homesick, he said, "The first thing I'm going to do when I get home is go to the beach with some beer and

watch the sunset—just me and my beer and God."
When Zack came home tonight, the music from
Eduardo's radio was bouncing off the walls. Zack's
comment: "I can tell we have a teenager in the house
again!"

Sunday, 25 January. Eduardo went to church with
us today. He wanted to go. I'm sure he sees it as a
cultural learning experience. He appeared interested in
every part of the worship service. He particularly liked
the music. He said, "This church is a happy place."
The better I get to know him, the more I sense he is a
caring and perceptive person. He is well-traveled and
more knowledgeable about the world than the average
American youth.

Friday, 30 January. Eduardo is still having adjustment problems. He gets homesick often, and during
those times he is moody and withdrawn. Being accustomed to much independence, he chafes at not being
allowed to drive. Zack takes him to school and I meet
him when school is out. Our life-style puzzles him. He
is amazed by how often we go to church and by how
long we *stay* once we get there! We are careful not to
force our values and faith upon him, yet he is curious
and asks a lot of questions. He has no concept of a
personal relationship with Christ. He said he wasn't
even sure he believed in God, although he has been
educated at Catholic schools.

Wednesday, 11 February. Eduardo has been here a
month. He seems to be over his homesickness. Now,
Zack and I are having adjustment problems. There is
no question this has been an intrusion into our lives.
There really was no way we could be prepared for all
the abrupt changes that have accompanied his coming.

Because of Eduardo's culture, he definitely considers women second-class citizens. He is a bit patronizing to me at times. He is not accustomed to cleaning his room or cleaning up the messes he makes. His room stays in a perpetual chaotic mess, which drives even me wild. He's also somewhat of a space cadet. He either forgets to take his house key with him, or he leaves it in the front door. He forgets to turn off burners and ovens. He assumes I will be available to meet his every need. I'm beginning to resent his attitude of taking me for granted. He often talks condescendingly about people and customs here as though we are very provincial (which we probably are!) and as though everything in Rio is superior.

Friday, 13 February. An emotional day. When I met Eduardo after school, he told me he had decided not to go on the church-sponsored, youth ski trip to Colorado. When I pressed him for a reason, he became very emotional and distraught. Finally, he told me. He feels rejected by our church youth. With much emotion he said, "They don't like me. They think I'm a bad person because I smoke and I like beer." Loudly and clearly has come the message from at least some of our church youth: "I'll love and accept you if you'll change and be like I am and think like I do and share my values." What a number we evangelicals have done on our youth. We haven't taught them how to separate the person from his actions, how to love unconditionally. I cried with Eduardo.

Tuesday, 17 February. Eduardo has changed his mind about the ski trip. He is going, after all. Something happened to change his mind, but I haven't a clue what it was, except I've been praying about the situation!

Friday, 20 March. The ski trip is happy history. Eduardo had a great time and now feels like one of the crowd. Having made friends with several of the boys from church, he is in high spirits. I wish I were. He is doing more things that bug me—making messes in the kitchen and not cleaning them up, becoming argumentative. Some things alarm me. He has met a much older Brazilian guy (a college student), and I'm certain they are drinking together. Eduardo resents the curfew we've given him. Being aware of cultural differences, we have tried to give Eduardo "space," but his "space" is interfering with our rest and peace of mind.

Wednesday, 1 April. School officials called today to inform me Eduardo has been placed on detention for excessively cutting class. *What next?* I'm ready to ship him home. I wonder, did we make a mistake in taking an exchange student?

Friday, 3 April. When I wrote my last entry, I asked, "What next?" I could hardly have imagined, after all the growing frustration, the "next" would be so wonderful! Tonight Eduardo became a Christian! Tonight, at a "Disciple Now" event for our church youth, Eduardo invited Christ into his life. We are about to burst with excitement. Through the past months, Eduardo has asked many questions about our beliefs, and we've tried to answer them by pointing him toward the person of Jesus, not toward Baptists or a creed. This is one of the happiest days of my life!

Monday, 13 April. Eduardo is really a changed young man. It is indescribably exciting to see the miracle of a transformed life. We are experiencing sweet fellowship with him now.

Sunday, 10 May. Eduardo was baptized today by Zack. We did not urge him to become a Baptist, but it was his wish to be baptized into our church. He was pretty nervous about the baptism. One of his good friends teased him before the service, saying, "You know, when we baptize foreigners, we hold them under longer!" Our church family has rejoiced with him and us. Eduardo has just one more month with us. There's much we want to do and experience together in these last days.

Sunday, 31 May. This was Eduardo's last day at church. It was pretty emotional. Our church youth have become his best friends. They just needed time. I was too hasty in judging them. Eduardo is having a tough time saying good-bye. Yesterday we had a big family get-together, and our kids brought gifts for Eduardo. Zack and I gave him a Bible and a rod and reel.

Wednesday, 3 June. This has got to be one of the saddest days of my life. Eduardo is gone. We drove him to the airport at noon, ate lunch together at the airport, then suddenly it was time for him to board his plane. He had said he wanted no serious speeches, so we talked of inconsequential things. We exchanged final hugs, then with a declaration to return someday and a big smile, he was gone. I'm back home, not believing how empty the house is. This morning, just before we left, Eduardo walked through the house for a last time. He went back into "his" room and said, "Good-bye, room." Then he said, "Well, that's it. Let's go." We've all three cried. I never dreamed I would feel this bereft when he left us. I've been touched, discomfited, enlightened, perplexed and enriched by Eduardo Paes. I wonder if we'll ever see him again? I believe we will. He will remain in my heart forever.

August, 1987. Today we received a cassette from Eduardo. We listened to it, laughing and crying, as once again his voice filled the house. He told us of his busy life back in school in Rio. He told us over and over how much he loved us and missed us. He said, "I couldn't say these things while I was there. It's very hard to express how I feel. But I'll never forget you and Denton, Texas." Who can know what God has in store for Eduardo? Who can say how many lives may be changed before God gets through with Eduardo Paes! His family has invited us to visit them in Rio.*

Could there be an Eduardo in your life? Is there a Connie in your life? I'm convinced the greatest need in Christian ministry is to be found *outside* the walls of the church. We rush hither and yon, playing church, getting all stirred up about which room our Sunday School class is assigned or whether or not the choir sings anthems we like or whether or not we liked the preacher's sermon, while all around us people are hurting and are unaware of the abundant life. If our worship does not send us out to minister to these hurting people, we have not truly worshiped.

Jesus said,

---

*In October 1987, Zack and I flew to Rio de Janeiro to visit Eduardo and his family. It was a joyful reunion, and we fell in love with his family. Now, they are planning to visit us!

You are the salt of the earth; but if the salt has become tasteless, how will it be made salty again? It is good for nothing anymore, except to be thrown out and trampled under foot by men. You are the light of the world. A city set on a hill cannot be hidden. Let your light shine before men in such a way that they may see your good works, and glorify your Father who is in heaven (Matt. 5:13-14, 15).

And in John 4:35, we find,

Do you not say, 'There are yet four months, and then comes the harvest?' Behold, I say to you, lift up your eyes, and look on the fields, that they are white for harvest.

Zack and I have not done nearly enough salting or lighting or sowing or harvesting. But I am motivated to do more by the words of the psalmist in Psalm 126:5-6.

Those who sow in tears shall reap with joyful shouting. He who goes to and fro weeping, carrying his bag of seed, shall indeed come again with a shout of joy, bringing his sheaves with him.

The harvest field may be within your extended family. If you work outside the home, the harvest field is where you work. The harvest field is in your neighborhood. It may be at the beauty shop, the grocery store, on an airplane.

It used to be almost impossible for me to talk about Jesus, except at church. I thought I had to be a great Bible scholar and be able to answer every question. I always felt guilty about how little I shared my faith, but I felt I would be a colossal failure (and drive people farther from the Lord) if I tried to talk to them about Him.

If that's how it is with you, be strengthened by the

words of Paul in 2 Timothy 1:7: "For God has not given us the spirit of fear; but of power, and of love, and of a sound mind" (KJV).

I first realized that God could use even the most simple witnessing attempts about twenty years ago. I was a young wife and mother, and was confronted with the need to share my faith while busily preparing our evening meal. Earlier in the day I had read in the newspaper an account of local teenagers being arrested for possession of drugs. They were released to the custody of their parents, but faced serious charges. All day the incident was in my mind. To this day, I distinctly remember every detail of that evening. I was standing at the kitchen sink, peeling potatoes, when it registered on me that one of the girls involved lived only a few blocks from our home. God impressed me with the thought: *You need to go talk to her.*

But, Lord, I thought, *I don't even know her... she would resent the intrusion of a stranger... she may not even be home... if she is home, her family will probably be eating at this time... besides I need to finish our meal.*

She's more important than cooking potatoes. Go.

I quit peeling potatoes, picked up my Bible, and called to eleven-year-old Kenny, "Take care of Carolyn and see that you both stay in the house. I'll be back soon, and Dad will be home any minute."

I knocked on the door of her home, feeling awkward, embarrassed, wondering if she would be home, wondering what to say. It seemed an eternity before the door opened. I was about to leave when she appeared at the door. She was at home alone.

I introduced myself and asked if I might come in. As I entered the home, I paused a moment, looking into her eyes, and the next thing I knew, my arms were around her, holding her. At first, all I could say was, "I don't know you, but I care about you, and I had to come." We sat on a sofa and began to talk. I listened to her, then told her of the greatest Friend in all the world Who loved her and Who would stand by her. We read some Scriptures together. I asked her if she would like to know Jesus Christ in a personal way, and to my amazement, she said yes! Right there, in the darkening shadows of the evening, sitting on a sofa in her living room, she asked Christ to come into her life.

A week later she joined a little church near her home and was warmly received by the members. She was placed on probation by the judge. The last I heard of her, she was faithfully attending church and blossoming in her new faith.

If your only friends are "church" friends, would you consider taking a step beyond your church? Admittedly, being salt can get us into some uncomfortable, even disquieting, situations but the results are more than worth the risks.

Not all my attempts to reach out to those outside the church have been successful. Some years ago I went to call on a lady who was not a member of any church. I had been told she was lonely and probably had many needs. Since she lived near us, I walked to her home. Thinking she might be more likely to receive me, a stranger, I introduced myself as a neighbor and the wife of a Baptist minister. She was quite articulate as she slammed the door shut: "I've known all the Baptists I care to know!"

At first I felt more than slightly offended and indignant. But as I walked home and considered her words, I laughed. If she'd given me a chance, I could have said, "Lady, sometimes I've felt exactly the same way!"

Lord, You are too wonderful! I can't begin to comprehend Your love. Thank You for all the people You've brought into our lives. Forgive us for the missed opportunities to be salt and light. Continue to push us out into your world, the REAL world. Show us how to be real. Keep teaching us how to love.

7

When You Discover
Other Staff Wives
(And Their Mates)
Are Human Too!

Discovering other staff wives and mates are human is a wonderful blessing. It frees us of the burden of being perfect!

The subject of staff relationships is a relatively new agenda because the staff wife is a relatively new breed. The *minister's wife*, or pastor's wife, has been with us at least since the Reformation! Correction. Make that since the first century. I just remembered that the apostle Peter had a wife. *The staff wife*, however, has gradually evolved during the past thirty years.

Many folk my age remember the day when most churches were staffed only by a pastor. A layman was "the singer" who led congregational music and maybe directed a choir. After World War II we saw the emergence of a new staff person who assisted the pastor. The support person was likely a combination man who "did" music, religious education, youth work—you name it!

Zack was a combination man for eight years. In his early years of ministry, he was the music director, the educational director, and the youth director, all rolled into one. In our first churches, he and I even typed and printed our Sunday bulletins, cranking them out on an old mimeograph machine early each Sunday morning. I

went through every Sunday morning worship service
with purple mimeograph ink on my hands!

Today is the era of the multiministerial church staff.
The staff wife today may be the wife of the pastor, the
associate pastor, the minister of education, the church
administrator, the minister of music, the minister to
youth, the minister to senior adults, the minister to single
adults, and the list goes on.

The expansion and diversification of church staffs and
the changing staff roles have created new problems for
wives searching for their niche, their identity. Building
and maintaining good staff relationships is not always
easy. The larger the church staff, the more personalities
with whom one must relate. Over and over at staff wives'
conferences I hear a familiar refrain: "I need help with
staff relationships. How can I handle a difficult problem
with another staff wife?" Or, I hear, "There are so many
inequities in the treatment of staff members at our
church. My husband feels discouraged and unappreciated. How can I help him handle this?"

I'm going to attempt to deal with this complex matter
from two perspectives: How the church body can help,
and the staff members' responsibilities.

A word to church members first. There is a deep need
for each staff person and his wife to feel loved and
affirmed. I make no apology for that need. Though we
serve because we love the Lord, all human beings need
to feel appreciated. The least word of affirmation is such a
blessing. Being remembered at Christmas with a Christmas card or receiving a little note of love and encouragement brings indescribable joy! Church members can do
much, through little things, to build up and edify their staff.
The little things, especially supportive words, are big things!

In many churches there is great disparity in the degrees of support and nurturing toward staff members from the church family. Some churches project the attitude that only the pastor (and maybe, the associate pastor) are the "called ones," while the rest of the staff is just salaried personnel hired to do a job. All church staff persons I know share a sense of divine calling to full-time ministry. All believe God called them to their places of service. A sensitive, caring church family can do much to help staff relations by its attitude toward staff. Not for one moment do I perceive church staff as "infallible persons who run the church." Quite the contrary, I wish there was less distinction between clergy and laity. I am simply asking for an attitude of prayerful support from the church toward all those called to lead.

Now, several words to staff wives:

Many staff wives (as well as their husbands) are carrying around some negative baggage because they have not come to terms with a reality of the church staff. The reality is: the pastor is the undershepherd of the church; the rest of the staff is support staff. True, all the members of the staff are partners in ministry, but the pastor has been called to shepherd the church. The support staff chose their areas of service and responded to their call knowing this reality. A big problem unique to the support staff and wives is the acceptance of this reality emotionally as well as mentally. One may give mental assent yet allow resentments to creep in when one sees the pastor receiving more salary, more "strokes," etc. Being the human creatures we are, from time to time we must deal with feelings of envy, competitiveness, and, yes, even jealousy.

How do we deal with negative, destructive feelings toward others on staff?

There are three options open to us. We can nurture those negative feelings and grow them into a full-blown, *serious* case of *resentment and hurt*. (We can cause serious divisions in the church by criticizing fellow staff members and by trying to gather our own "following.") Or, we can repress the negative feelings, denying their existence, and wonder why we are so unhappy. Or, we can face them honestly and ethically.

Facing them honestly means acknowledging in total honesty to the Lord the name of the problem. Is it envy, jealousy, rejection, hurt, anger? Begin by being honest with yourself and the Lord. You can tell Him exactly what the problem is and exactly what your feelings are. He already knows anyway. Pray about the difficult situation and pray *for* the one with whom you're having problems. Ask the Lord to show you where *you* have been at fault—perhaps you could have been more understanding or more aware of the other person's needs. Perhaps you are just plain envious because you seek more power or recognition.

Facing them ethically means not talking about staff members to others. Staff wives (and their husbands) *must* be loyal to their pastor and his wife. Likewise, the pastor and wife must be loyal and supportive of the support staff. This is the only ethical attitude and action to practice. If for some reason, in extremely rare situations, you believe a fellow staff person is guilty of some immorality or unethical practice, or if there is a serious difference in point of view, you should go to that person with your differences. *Do not discuss it with others.* If you have any problem with a fellow staff member or wife, go to him or her (it is wise to have a third, objective party present) and prayerfully, openly, redemptively discuss the problem. This is the biblical way, and is the only way to harmonious relations. Avoid being drawn into a conversation criticizing a colleague. Attacking a colleague is not only unprofessional, it's unchristian. The apostle Paul made it pretty clear when he wrote in Ephesians 4:32:

> Stop being mean, bad-tempered, and angry. Quarrelling, harsh words, and dislike of others should have no place in your lives. Instead, be kind to each other, tenderhearted, forgiving one another, just as God has forgiven you because you belong to Christ (TLB).

If you are a staff wife having trouble loving another staff wife, remember she is human, too. If you are critical and jealous, you can hardly expect that one to respond to you as best friend!

But what if you've done everything you can to be friends with a staff wife and you continue to be rejected? The only successful formula I know is to continue to pray for that person! (Does this sound familiar?) I believe God will either change the relationship or show you how to handle it in love. He may move one of you!

Both the pastor and his wife can do much to create the attitude among staff of a shared ministry, of a sense of partnership in ministry. Staff retreats that include mates are excellent ways to foster growing, positive staff relationships. The pastor's wife can help relieve pressure on the other staff wives by being her own person. She has a wonderful opportunity, as pastor's wife, to reach out to the other staff wives and lead the way in creating a harmonious spirit. Having staff-wives' get-togethers for birthdays and other special occasions helps wives know one another better.

Close friendships can, and often do, develop between staff wives. Because they share common problems, they can provide a bulwark of support for each other. I have been profoundly influenced by fellow staff wives who have not only befriended me, but who modeled before me lives of graciousness and dignity and good humor.

However, it is not necessary for staff wives to be "best friends" with each other. It's OK, when interests and jobs and ages are varied, for each to do her own thing and, to a certain extent, go her own way. Staff wives can still enjoy getting together for special occasions and can still *be supportive of one another.*

Have I ever experienced broken fellowship with another staff wife? Of course I have! Let me tell you about LaVon and me.

LaVon was the beautiful and talented wife of our minister to youth. We were both young, outgoing, and actively involved in church. We became good friends. One Sunday when several families gathered to share Sunday dinner, LaVon and I exchanged sharp words. Interestingly, I cannot remember what caused our quarrel. I only remember how miserable I felt. That night at church we carefully avoided each other. Naturally, I felt defensive and tried to convince myself I had been misunderstood.

I slept little Sunday night and continued to feel depressed the next day. It rained Monday evening as I drove to a night class, but my mood was darker than the skies. I couldn't concentrate on the class, and left early. Driving home, I began to pray. As I prayed, the tears came. "Lord," I begged, "please restore my friendship with LaVon. I can't bear this broken relationship."

The Lord didn't have to speak out loud for me to get

the message. *You know what you should do. You need to go to LaVon and apologize.*

"But, Lord, that's awfully hard to do!"

The knot inside got bigger. Finally I could stand it no longer. While still driving, I reached a decision. "All right, Lord, if You'll go with me and prepare the way, I'll go. I'll go tonight."

I stopped by home first to check on the kids and to tell them where I would be. As I prepared to leave for the second time that evening, the doorbell rang.

Standing on my front porch was LaVon! She had come to me! We literally fell into each other's arms, and laughing and crying together, we began to express words of love and forgiveness. It was an evening I'll never forget. What a lesson I learned!

Our Lord most certainly is in the business of healing broken relationships when we yield ourselves and the relationship to Him. And when He puts a life or a relationship back together, He does a wonderful job! LaVon's and my friendship became stronger than ever. We have had the unusual experience of serving on two church staffs together. Today, though miles apart, our two families continue to be close friends. It does bother me a little that she has stayed young and attractive, and I've aged! However, she has two sons in college and a young teenage daughter still at home. She will no doubt age quickly in the next few years!

I don't intend to imply that it is always easy to prevent or solve serious problems in staff relationships. Lynn's husband, a minister of education, has served their church faithfully and well for many years with few and minimal salary adjustments. Recently the personnel committee of the church created a new staff position and brought in a new man, giving him a significantly higher salary, and placing him in authority over the rest of the support staff. It seems to Lynn and her husband that the new man has aggressively and authoritatively "taken over" and immediately created many changes. Lynn talked to me about her husband's feelings of discouragement. "He feels so unappreciated," she said. "And it's hard not to feel resentment."

How can you help your husband when he is discouraged? Ultimately, all you can do is pray for him, pray with him, love him, remind him of his strengths, allow him to talk about his feelings but don't encourage him to dwell on them, and give the situation to the Lord. If you and your mate are experiencing a low time of frustration and discouragement, it helps to get away from it all, even briefly. We can't run away from our problems, but we can certainly put some distance between them and us, often gaining a fresh perspective.

There are no end of Scriptures applicable to church staff relations. The first passage that comes to mind is Philippians 2:3-7.

> Do nothing from selfishness or empty conceit, but with humility of mind let each of you regard one another as more important than himself; do not merely look out for your own personal interests, but also for the interests of others. Have this attitude in yourselves which was also in Christ Jesus, who, although He existed in the form of God, did not regard equality with God a thing to be grasped, but emptied Himself, taking the form of a bond-servant.

The phrase, "taking the form of a bond-servant," says it all. That's talking about taking on the mind-set of serving instead of being served, of yielding instead of seeking one's own way. Though some of us struggle more than others with growth in this area, I suspect the desire for recognition is at the root of most staff relationship problems. I can't be too critical of James and John for seeking prestigious positions in Christ's kingdom when I realize I'm often guilty of the same thing. They completely failed to understand Jesus' words, "If anyone wants to be first, he shall be last of all, and servant of all" (Mark 9:35), and had to be reminded by Jesus, "For even the Son of Man did not come to be served, but to serve" (10:45). I, too, often need to be reminded of those words.

Competition among Christians for status and recognition is nothing new! James and John, who knew Jesus intimately, succumbed to the temptation to be self-seeking, and we modern-day Christians still battle the same temptation. Remembering Jesus' words, "It is not so among you" (v. 43), would improve many staff relationships.

Relating to others in a spirit of Christian love is always a challenge. Other than family relationships, those which present the greatest challenge are relationships at work. Naturally, when we work closely with people day after day we become aware of their weaknesses as well as their strengths. Generally, we accept the irritating little habits and eccentricities of personality and changing moods of family members, but we're less tolerant of those with whom we work.

Thank goodness my fellow staff wives (and their mates) are not perfect! I wouldn't be able to relate to them at all!

Relationships with staff-wife colleagues have provided some of the greatest joys of being "in ministry." Were it not for wiser, more spiritually mature staff wives who lovingly and patiently encouraged and affirmed me, I would probably have failed more, despaired more. Sometimes, fellow staff wives helped me shape up. I've never forgotten Dorothy Noel's matter-of-fact voice saying, "Nancy, you're too much of a reactor. If you're mad, sad, or whatever, the whole world knows it!" She helped me learn more about discretion and patience. Dorothy and Wanda Hultgren taught me about hanging in there when life hurts, about being one's own person. Margaret Jordan reached out to me, a young staff wife, and modeled a caring, sweet spirit.

Thank goodness all staff wives are not only human, but wonderfully different from one another. Isn't it wonderful that they all have varied gifts and personalities?! They don't all sing solos, they don't all play the piano, they don't all teach, they don't all make incredible casseroles, they aren't all perfect housekeepers (I just threw that one in to affirm wives like me), and they don't all agree with me! *Vive la difference!*

Heavenly Father, thank You for the beautiful staff wives you've placed in my path. And thank you for Sue, Margaret, Marcia, Joan, and Glenda, who have to serve with me right now. Give them an abundance of patience, perseverance, and tolerance.

8 Rejoice Always?

We were going to be late to Sunday School—again. My minister husband and I were not speaking as we drove to church.

The roast had burned while I was motivating the kids, ages ten and six, to get their acts together. The collar button had popped off Zack's only ironed dress shirt, and all my stockings had runs. No matter how well you plan ahead for Sunday morning, Murphy's Law dictates that all your stockings will sprout runs. Just as we were going out the door, the dog darted out and made her daily flight for freedom. I ran after her, lurching precariously on high heels, yelling things that entertained the neighbors. Actually, it was a rather normal Sunday morning.

On the way to church I tried to compose my scattered thoughts and focus on the devotional I was to give in Adult 3 ("Celebrate Family"), but all that registered was an argument coming from the backseat.

"It's your turn to wash Sunday dishes."

"Is not."

"Is, too. I did it last Sunday."

"Did not."

At that point, I glared at both children and threatened,

"If you two don't hush, I'll cook liver for dinner! Now let me have some peace and quiet."

Moments later I heard, "Mom, he's staring at me again!"

It was mornings like that when Zack understood the position of the Catholic Church in forbidding a married clergy.

I rushed into the church and hurried down the hall toward Adult 3, extremely agitated, certain every eye in the church would be focused on the run in my stocking. I happened to pass Mrs. Pederson, and I didn't look cheerful.

She was waiting for me after church.

"Nancy, Dear," she whispered in the hushed voice one uses to denote extreme concern, "I'm worried about you. Are you all right? You don't seem *happy*."

By then I was able to laugh and say, "When you saw me this morning, I wasn't happy! I was ready to shoot a husband and two children. But I'm OK now. Thanks for asking."

We all know the proper staff wife is always cheerful and happy, no matter what. Right? Hardly! Where in the world did we get the notion ministers and ministers' wives were not allowed to get discouraged or depressed? Who put forth the idea that if you are frustrated or hurt or, God forbid, angry, you're obviously not spiritual enough?! It doesn't matter if you've been cheerful and sweet and spiritual for forty-seven straight Sundays, let one Sunday morning roll around when all you-know-what breaks loose, and you are certain to meet Mrs. Pederson in the hall. Her soul sisters exist in every church. They are the ones who pat you on the arm, no matter what the crisis, and say, "Honey, if you'll just pray about it, you'll feel better." (It's good to express concern, not good to proffer platitudes. Hurting people need love, and it is often best expressed with a simple touch or hug.)

Admittedly, the Sunday morning scene just described is hardly a life-shaking crisis. It points out, however, that ministers' families are not immune to the same stresses experienced by others. We all have "down" times when we're temporarily disheartened or momentarily discouraged.

Or, we may find ourselves in a situation so overwhelming that we don't know how to pray. Sometimes, in our humanness, we get to the end of our rope and don't know how to tie a knot and hang on. I am well aware of the Scripture in 1 Thessalonians 5:16 saying, "Rejoice always." But, if we're honest, we're not always able to rejoice.

Even the most stable and spiritually minded people get depressed. Martin Luther, Charles H. Spurgeon, and Peter Marshall are among a host of spiritual giants who had bouts with depression.

I know depression. It sneaked in the back door once and settled in before I recognized its presence. For a long while it wrapped around me like a heavy coat. It took on many forms. It was a weight so ponderous, even ordinary activities required great effort. It was physical pain, an aching in my chest. Most of all, it was deep sadness, an inexplicable sadness that triggered constant tears. No one, it seemed, not even my husband, really understood how I felt. I wanted to escape the world.

Depression can be brought on by:

- exhaustion
- physical illness (a prolonged illness, or various physiological causes such as hormonal changes)

- a spiritual void
- disillusionment with others
- repeated rejection
- unavoidable problems and crises (the loss of a loved one or the suffering of loved ones)
- chemical causes such as medication (I have a friend who suffered severe depression after being administered an anesthetic for surgery.)
- major turning points and changes in life
- deeply embedded, repressed anger

This chapter is about getting through the bad times. It is a sharing of practical ways to *work through* those tough times to the place where once again you can rejoice. Assuredly, I will be primarily a synthesizer, blending together the ideas of others that have served me well in my own stormy pilgrimage.

"Rejoice always." There it is. Right there in God's Word. It plainly means, doesn't it, that no matter what happens, we're to smile from ear to ear and say, "Hallelujah! If life hands you a lemon, just make lemonade"? Or does it?

Let's remove our super-spiritual robes and drop our religious clichés for just a minute and answer this question honestly. Do you *really* rejoice when a friend has betrayed you, or your mate has misunderstood and wrongly criticized you, or a teenage child has broken your heart, or you've messed up badly, or your marriage is falling apart, or your husband's job has just been terminated, or you are standing at the grave of a loved one?

What exactly did Paul mean when he said, "Rejoice always," and is it possible to rejoice at all times? Was he telling us to rejoice *for* the bad things that happen? Some insist he was. Some godly people whose writings I respect have maintained that we are to thank God *for* everything. I cannot believe, however, that God wants us to thank Him for evil. I cannot thank Him for child abuse, for rape, for oppression, for murder, for starving humanity. I *do* believe we can make our way to the place of being able to thank Him and rejoice in Him *in spite* of the circumstances of life.

I heard a recent, beautiful illustration of rejoicing in the Lord in spite of circumstances. Steve and Anne Seaberry, foreign missionaries appointed to Zaire, were forced to evacuate their mission post when their city fell to angry, rioting soldiers. They had just begun to see evidence of exciting growth when their ministry was abruptly halted. They had to leave behind most of their possessions. Trying to sort through a melange of emotions, Steve expressed my theology when he said, "I cannot rejoice in the destruction of the city, in the raping of women, in the looting of homes, in the hindrance to our work; but I rejoice in the Lord—in His miraculous Presence and Protection and Guidance. Our family will never doubt the reality of the Lord!"

For more than the past decade, I've been hearing from several quarters a concept I call the "Make Lemonade" philosophy. This one says, "Don't worry, be happy no matter what." This rather shallow statement to someone who has just experienced tragedy is propagated by those who always smile brightly and appear to sort of bounce through each day saying something like, "I just praise the Lord because my washing machine broke down and flooded the house!" I know of a young woman who lost her husband suddenly and prematurely, who on the day of his death, as friends gathered around, said,

"This is the happiest day of my life, because my husband is now with the Lord."

I have a big problem with this philosophy. I don't believe it's honest, healthy, or biblical. Jesus wept at the tomb of Lazarus. Is it too difficult to believe that our Lord was *grieving*, that He was hurting because His friend was dead and because His other friends, Mary and Martha, were suffering?

There's another prevalent philosophy in certain spiritual circles, similar to the "Make Lemonade" one. This is the "If You're Just Spiritual Enough" philosophy. This one says, "God doesn't intend for His children to suffer—to be poor or sick or to fail tests or to get overdrawn at the bank. If you are spiritual enough, you won't have problems."

Charles Swindoll, in *Three Steps Forward Two Steps Back*, has much to say about this. "Christians need to be told that difficulty and pressure are par for the course. No amount of biblical input or deeper-life conferences or super-victory seminars will remove our human struggle. God promises no bubble of protection, no guaranteed release from calamity."[1] He goes on to insist, "[The process of growing and learning] is sometimes painful, often slow, and occasionally downright awful! It's like taking three steps forward and two steps back."[2]

So, if you'll hang in here with me, I want us to examine some principles I believe will be both helpful and biblical for getting through those times when we feel unloved, unappreciated, angry, resentful, hurt, when we want to run away, when we think the sun will not shine again.

First, *acknowledge your feelings honestly to God*. Give yourself permission to be human, to talk to God in *real* talk. Tell Him exactly how you feel. Tell Him you are angry, frustrated, lonely, hurt, sad, and why. He won't be surprised or shocked. Since He knows our every attitude as well as action, we might as well admit it all, without any reservations, to Him. If you hate someone, tell Him. If you're angry at God, tell Him. He can handle it. Many of God's most choice servants told Him in no uncertain terms how they were feeling!

Listen to Elijah in 1 Kings 19:4 when he was fleeing from Jezebel: " 'I've had enough,' he told the Lord. 'Take away my life' " (TLB).

Listen to Jeremiah in Jeremiah 20:15,17-18: "Cursed be the day that I was born! Cursed be the man that brought my father the news that a son was born. Oh! that I had died within my mother's womb!... Why was I ever born?" (TLB).

What do you say to someone like Elijah and Jeremiah? Cheer up? If life hands you a lemon, just make lemonade? These guys were being absolutely honest with God. They weren't defying God or rejecting Him. They were admitting their despair.

Throughout the Bible we read of God's saints experiencing depression *and their admission of it to God.* Healing is not possible until we face God honestly with our problems. Catherine Marshall said that coming before Jesus, stripped of pretensions, in total honesty, is not easy but it's the only way. Naked honesty with *yourself,* as well as with God, is absolutely essential in order for healing to begin to take place.

So, in the dark times, *keep talking to God.* Start by admitting how you really feel. That was the first step up and out for Elijah and Jeremiah.

Next, accept the fact that problems and suffering are an inescapable part of this life. That's not being fatalistic.

That's accepting truth. We don't like to hear this, because no one likes to suffer. We are all so frantically in pursuit of happiness, we Christians have lost sight of why we are here. The television character, Father Mulcahy on "M*A*S*H," reminds us: "God didn't put us here for a pat on the back. He put us here so that He could be here in us, reaching out to help others."

Swindoll insists that our great God is not obligated to make us comfortable. He says, "Surprising though it may be to most people, the Bible teaches that our major purpose in life is not to be comfortable and happy but to glorify and serve God."[3]

This idea is reinforced by Paul Billheimer in his book *Don't Waste Your Sorrows*. He expresses the ideas that all life is intended to be a pathway to God, and all is for the purpose of character training. No suffering is purposeless. Billheimer asserts that there is no character without suffering, and that suffering, triumphantly accepted, delivers one from self-centeredness and frees one to love.[4]

That's the whole idea of Romans 8:28. I like it from *The Living Bible*: "And we know that all that happens to us is working for our good if we love God and are fitting into His plans."

Suffering is inevitable. Even though God does not cause our suffering, He permits it in order to strengthen us, mature us, draw us closer to Him. Dr. Warren Hultgren often says, "In God's army, only the wounded serve best." He also contends, "Christianity doesn't explain suffering, but it tells us how to deal with it."

We will be misunderstood. Our mate, our children, other family members, people in the church, people with whom we work—all will hurt us at some time or another. We will be disappointed and disillusioned. We will face rejection. We may face tragedy. Accept suffering as part of the human experience. *Real* Christianity is a struggle. If you doubt it, reread *The Pilgrim's Progress.*

Third, retreat, but not into a vacuum, not into a closet of self-pity. Withdraw into a quiet place with God's Word, and begin to allow His Spirit to speak to you through His Word. Seek Him. Listen to Him.

Catherine Marshall said whenever she came to Jesus with a needy spirit, ready to listen to Him and to receive what He had for her, He met her at her point of need.

During this time of retreat, *know that God is real and present whether you feel His presence or not.* His Word says He will never forsake us. Accept that God's presence is not determined by our feelings. We tend to evaluate everything, particularly our spiritual progress, by our feelings; and our feelings are not a reliable measuring stick. Often I don't feel very spiritual!

I have never forgotten a time, nearly twenty-five years ago, when I was a sponsor at a church camp. It seemed everyone else was experiencing a spiritual high, but I couldn't seem to feel any special emotion. The more I tried to manufacture a huge spiritual feeling, the less spiritual I felt! Toward the close of the camp, I approached the camp pastor and expressed concern for myself. I said, "I'm beginning to wonder if I'm a Christian. I don't *feel* like a Christian is supposed to feel."

I still remember his reply, "Nancy, how is a Christian supposed to feel?" He went on to give me some wonderful advice about trusting God even when I was experiencing a dry spell of feelings.

God does not seem bent toward giving me many emotional spiritual experiences. He knows I would probably talk or write about the experiences and magnify myself!

Most of my life, He has seemed to say, *Trust Me and walk with Me and obey Me, whether you are feeling any great explosion of joy or not.*

A few years ago I wrote in a journal, "I'm trying to reach out to God, to feel His presence. I know He wants me to walk in faith anyway, but I so desperately want to feel the reality of His presence in my life I've cried out to Him in my need, I've confessed sin, yet still the joy I seek escapes me. Why do I struggle so? Why is it I can think I've surrendered all to Jesus (and sincerely mean it), then moments later be right back trying to fight my own battles?"

The next day I wrote, "Today I've decided I'm going to serve Jesus regardless of my feelings. I told Him so. It was no big emotional deal, but I feel at peace." And shortly after I wrote those last words, joy did come. It rather slipped up on me quietly, without fanfare. I simply felt a deep sense of happiness and serenity and certainty of the reality of Christ.

During your time of retreat, draw strength from His Word. So many Scriptures particularly speak to us in times of discouragement. Consider Isaiah 40:27-29 from *The Living Bible*:

> How can you say that the Lord doesn't see your troubles and isn't being fair? Don't you yet understand? Don't you know by now that the everlasting God, . . . never grows faint or weary? . . . He gives power to the tired and worn out and strength to the weak.

And what about Isaiah 41:13? "For I, the Lord your God, hold your right hand; it is I who say to you, 'Fear not, I will help you'" (RSV).

Did you catch that? He holds each of us by the hand!

When six-year-old Amy and I, or three-year-old Molly and I, cross the street or walk through the shopping mall, I hold them tightly by the hand. With their little hands in mine, they are led in the right direction and protected from harm or evil. How could we fail to be comforted by His Word that says, "Don't be blown away. I'm holding your hand! I'll help you!"?

Other passages that have comforted me time after time are Isaiah 26:3; Psalms 27:14; 145:19.

During this retreat, relinquish your pain to the Lord. I mean, quit nursing it. For years (I'm embarrassed to admit how many), I asked God to free me of a resentment and hurt locked in my heart, but I wouldn't turn loose of it. One day during meditation, I felt God saying to me, *You have not been freed of the burden of hurt and resentment because you haven't wanted to give it up. You've wanted to feel sorry for yourself.* In that moment, I gave the burden to Him, and when I'm tempted to pick it back up, I remember: it's no longer mine, I gave it to the Lord. His power to heal and restore is real!

Then, while still in retreat, begin to thank and praise Him for all He has done. Recall everything you possibly can that God has done for you, both past and present. Remember the past crises He has brought you through. Remember answered prayers. Thank Him for the little things as well as the big. Do you have enough to eat? Do you have loving friends? How long has it been since you've thanked Him? As you begin to thank Him and dwell on His goodness, your spirit will begin to be warmed and encouraged. Praising and thanking God causes us to take our eyes off self and focus on Him.

Absolutely refuse to let negative thinking destroy an attitude of thankfulness. I'm reminded of a night when

our three-year-old son was saying his nightly prayers. He
thanked God for just about everything. After naming all
the family members and pets, he started naming everything else he could remember. He said, "And thank you,
God, for horses and cows and sheeps and elephants and
begrillas (gorillas)." There was a long pause, then, his
whole attitude changed as he added, "God, why did you
make begrillas and snakes?" Through the years, we've
smiled at his childish questioning of God, at the way his
thanksgiving turned into a complaint when he began to
consider the gorillas and snakes! The gorillas and snakes
are out there, but don't dwell on them!

Cultivate a thankful spirit. By the time our daughter
was three, she was practicing this principle. She never
liked to go to bed. To lessen resistance to bedtime, as I
tucked her in I encouraged her to recall all the happy
things of the day and thank God for them. One night after
we'd said her prayers, as I was leaving her room, I heard
her quivery voice saying, "And thank you, God, for not
nuthin' to get me when Mommy turns out the light."

Praise Him for all the good things He has done, is
doing, and will do. But we can't stay in retreat forever.

Next, do a good thing for someone else, and do a
happy thing for yourself. For a time, turn your thoughts
from yourself and do a thoughtful act for another. Write
that note of encouragement or congratulations or sympathy. Make that telephone call or visit to one who is lonely.
Bake or make something for someone else. Give something away to someone who is in need. There are also
positive benefits in doing a happy thing for yourself. Give
yourself permission to pamper yourself. Take a day off to
read a good book, go walking, do something fun with a
friend. Believe me, the rest of the universe will not be

thrown into cosmic shock if you leave some things un-
done and give yourself a holiday from responsibility. Part
of our problem as women is that we feel *too responsible*
for everything and everyone. Relax a little.

Last, continue spending daily time in prayer. I hope I
have not implied at any time that prayer is of minor
importance to me. Clichés about prayer bother me. But
prayer has come to be so much a part of my everyday life
I cannot imagine how people face life without it. So much
has been said and written about prayer—how to pray,
when to pray, the results of prayer, why God doesn't
answer prayer—I could hardly add a new perspective on
prayer. I can only add my affirmation, based on personal
experience, that God responds to prayer. That Almighty
God desires us to come into His presence and talk to Him
is awesome. In my prayer life, He has responded to
everything from the big and heavy and life-changing to
the seemingly little and insignificant. I didn't say He has
always given the answer I wanted. His answers have
been *yes, no,* and *trust Me with it.* Our daughter grew up
saying, "Alls I know is . . ." Well, "alls I know is," earnest
prayer—even when I don't see the exact results I'm
seeking—always strengthens and changes me.

These steps do not comprise a miraculous cure-all for
depression. Even to hint at such would be ridiculously
simplistic. Clinical depression or the grief following loss of
loved ones or deep psychological scarring require more
than a few steps up and out. If severe depression persists,
I would recommend seeing a medical doctor and, perhaps, a psychotherapist. At the time in my life when I
experienced a long period of depression, I was enor-
mously helped both by a simple medication that correc-
ted a chemical imbalance *and* by professional therapy.

Please don't deny yourself professional psychotherapy because of some erroneous idea it is a stigma or "unspiritual" to receive help from a psychologist or psychiatrist. All of us would at times benefit from good counseling. *The healthy person is the one who admits his need for help.*

> It is often the most spiritually healthy and advanced among us who are called on to suffer in ways more agonizing than anything experienced by the more ordinary. Great leaders, when wise and well, are likely to endure degrees of anguish unknown to the common man. Conversely, it is the unwillingness to suffer emotional pain that usually lies at the very root of emotional illness. Those who fully experience depression, doubt, confusion, and despair may be infinitely more healthy than those who are generally certain, complacent, and self-satisfied. The denial of suffering is, in fact, a better definition of illness than its acceptance[5]

Dr. M. Scott Peck insists it is more emotionally healthy to recognize a need for professional help and seek it than to let false pride keep us from a light-shedding process. Good psychotherapy *is* a light-shedding process.

Years ago, before experiencing severe depression, I began putting together the ideas expressed in this chapter. Confidently secure in my ability to *teach others* how to weather the storms of life, I led numerous conferences on dealing with depression. Little did I suspect how I would be challenged to follow my own advice. Through the process of writing this book, I have walked with loved ones through divorce, life-threatening illness and accidents, and through painful recoveries. I have felt rage, resentment, confusion, rejection, and grief.

Hear me carefully at this point. God did not cause my

suffering, but He certainly said to me in the midst of it: *Do you really believe what you've been teaching? Do you really believe I'm big enough to handle this?* I remember one night, during my darkest hour, when my rage could be repressed no longer, I walked out into the backyard and screamed and shook my fist at God. Can you possibly imagine what our incredible, loving God did? He wrapped His compassionate arms around me and ministered to me! In the hour of my greatest need, He made His Presence known to me and bathed me in love. I will never again doubt His Presence.

That night, after experiencing my deepest pain, I experienced my highest joy! As I responded to His tender love, I was able to *rejoice* in Him. That's what 1 Thessalonians 5:16 is all about. I can rejoice and thank God that suffering has brought me closer to Him and made me better able to identify with the suffering of others. That night, as tears of pain gave way to tears of joy, I was able to say for the first time, "Lord, I truly love You more than anyone or anything else."

Years ago during a sermon by a visiting preacher, I wrote this quote in my Bible: "I'm not so sure God is as interested in answering all our questions about pain and suffering as He is in giving us a fresh revelation of Himself. Nothing is really good or bad until God gets through with it."

Trials, small and gigantic, will continue to be with us. Stress is an inevitable part of daily life, partly due to our own making, and partly because Satan's goal is to frustrate us and keep us from joy. But Jesus says He has come that we might have (right now in this life) *abundant life.* After telling us to abide in Him, Jesus said, "These things have I spoken to you that My joy may be in you, and that your joy may be made full" (John 15:11).

Now that the kids are grown, it's easy for Zack and me to get off to church on Sunday mornings. It's easy for me to arrive at church with a serene, pleasant disposition, most of the time. Unless, of course, a not-so-serene church member has telephoned late Saturday night or early Sunday morning, or I've forgotten to pick up Zack's shirts at the laundry and my new pair of stockings sprang a run, or my hormones are doing weird things.

My prayer at these, and all times is:

Lord, there's so much to learn about You and Your way, a lifetime of study and communion with You is not enough. Thank You for continuing to teach me. Thank You for Your patient and sustaining affirmation. Help me to be understanding and supportive when others around me are hurting. Thank You for always restoring my joy!

9 Starting Over

Evidently, the writer of Ecclesiastes had just experienced a move to a new church when he wrote, "A time to cast away stones, and a time to gather stones together; a time to embrace, and a time to refrain from embracing; A time to get, and a time to lose; a time to keep, *and a time to cast away.*" (Eccl. 3:5-6, KJV, author's italics)

We've done a lot of casting away, particularly from the attic and the refrigerator, during each move. Zack is convinced I would never clean out the refrigerator if we didn't move. Close friends could not understand why we left Tulsa. After nine years, our refrigerator and closets were in such disrepute, we had to move.

Do you know why it is so tough starting a new work in a new church? The new church doesn't know right off what a wonderful family has come their way! You have to start all over again gaining acceptance, establishing new relationships, finding your place in the new environment.

Change is the common denominator of most staff wives. If you have never moved to a new church or do not anticipate moving, read this chapter anyway. It has to do with much more than making a move. Actually, it's about embracing change, about building new relationships while nurturing the old.

Making a move is always traumatic. Uprooting, leaving friends, facing the unknown, starting over in a new community is rough whether you are young or old or in-between. The older you are and the longer your tenure at your former church, the more difficult it is to change and adjust. A move is stressful for any family, not just families of church staffers, but once again the very nature of our husbands' work may impose extra stress during a move. The new staff family is always closely observed, and first impressions upon church members may become lasting ones.

Through all the trauma of getting the utilities turned on, discovering the movers damaged your grandmother's antique table, feeling overwhelmed by matching names to faces, and trying to find the box where you packed the coffeepot, you must be "putting forth your best foot." That means when Mrs. Jones drops by with a casserole and you open the door to greet her and your cat or dog, terrified by the new surroundings, dashes off into the unknown, you cannot swear.

Because uprooting is high on the list of stress factors, I think a discussion of it is *apropos*. Even when a move is eagerly anticipated, it is always accompanied by anxiety. Now, psychologists are acknowledging that moving takes a heavy emotional toll on families. Following a move, it is not unusual for the wife, and particularly the children, to experience feelings of loss and depression, resentment, and even anger.

This chapter addresses ways to cope when you have to start over after a move or after any major change.

Housing has become a critical issue and a major cause of stress. The day of the church-owned parsonage is almost history. (Thank goodness! We lived in a parsonage twice. The first one was perfect for our family. But the second left much to be desired. I tried to make the best of it, thinking we had no alternative. When we left to accept a position in another church, Zack's successor and his wife took one look at the parsonage and announced they would not live there. The church promptly bought them a new home!) Sagging economies and recession have placed heavy financial burdens on many of God's ministers. At this moment, hundreds of dedicated ministers, having followed God's call to new fields of service, are paying double for housing while waiting for former homes to sell. The stress on the family, both emotional and financial, is enormous. Sometimes, the former house never sells, leaving the family with no equity with which to purchase another. Somehow, I believe an aware and caring congregation can help the minister's family work through this relatively new problem brought on by depressed markets.

Responding to God's call to a new work is a step in faith. Everytime we've stepped out in faith, God has shown us new dimensions of His power and provision. He hasn't always answered our prayers exactly as we anticipated, but He has always provided our needs. And, in His graciousness, He has provided some of my wants that made the adjustment a little easier! For instance, about a year before our last move, we built a long-yearned-for arbor over the back porch. I loved that arbor! Almost every evening I sat in our swing under that beautiful arbor and felt the cares of the day slip away. I thought of it as my special place. And then we moved away! Part of my grief in leaving Tulsa was leaving our arbor. This may seem like a silly, inconsequential thing, but that arbor represented a sort of haven for me, and leaving it symbolized leaving the security of my known world. Would you believe, the *first* house shown to us, as we began to look for a new home, had a wonderful arbor over the back porch!? Would you believe, the owners reduced their asking price, making the house affordable for us!

The most practical advice I've found on surviving a move (other than my own, of course!) is in *Tips for Ministers and Mates.* Author Mary Bess points out the need of dwelling on the positive aspects of a move.

- the opportunity to get rid of accumulated clutter;
- having a wardrobe that is "new" to the new church;
- the opportunity to make new friends and experience new growth.[1]

Recognizing it takes about a year to get oriented to new surroundings, I'd like to emphasize seven guidelines for making it through that trying first year.

First, if you have children still living at home, give them top priority. Devote much time and attention to them. Children suffer the most in our moves. Some children are deeply scarred emotionally by moves. I realize now how miserably I failed to help our daughter adjust to a move midway through her fifth grade year. Absorbed in my own adjustment, I failed to see the pain of a little girl whose grief over leaving friends was as acute and real as my own. I assumed a ten-year-old could adjust easily and make new friends. Carolyn changed from a happy, secure, outgoing child to an insecure and unhappy one. During the first year after our move, she became literally unable to make a decision about what to wear. She often cried, begging to stay home from school. She eventually pulled through the trauma, but I know her pain could have been eased if I had been more perceptive. A thousand times I've yearned to be able to go back, to relive those years.

Second, refrain from talking about your former church in the sense of making comparisons. Don't cling to the past. We all recognize the wisdom of this advice. We just don't always practice it! It is not the best way to win new friends by saying, "When we were at . . . we did such and such." Recognize that every church is unique and look upon the new ways of doing things as an opportunity for growth. In our early days of ministry, I was slow to learn this valuable lesson. In my immaturity, I couldn't turn loose of a former, extraordinarily loving church family. Needless to say, I was seriously hindered in forming new friendships. This doesn't mean we should abandon former friends. Friendships can and should be nurtured for a lifetime. It takes energy and time to build new friendships and maintain old ones, but the dividends are priceless.

Third, give yourself time to adjust before assuming new church responsibilities. Refrain from rushing in and accepting leadership positions. Taking on jobs that require preparation add pressure when you are already overloaded with stress related to the move. It takes a little longer this way for people to realize how talented and wonderful you are, but they'll eventually learn!

Fourth, build bridges to the other staff wives. There is no unwritten law requiring you to be "best friends" with fellow staff wives. The fact that your husbands' jobs had brought you together does not mean you will share common interests or have personalities that are naturally attracted to one another. However, good staff relationships are imperative. When you are adjusting to a new church, work at building good relationships with the other staff wives.

Fifth, allow yourself to develop at least one interest or hobby or friendship outside the church. And keep growing by developing new interests. Be open to opportunities for growth. My interests have been tennis and writing. One staff wife I know joins garden clubs. One went back to school and took a computer course. Another sews and does home decorating projects. Another makes and sells wonderful country craft creations. But you don't have to be "crafty." The important thing is to have an interest outside your church activities. That interest may simply be reading or spending time by yourself, doing what you want to do.

Sixth, find a heart friend. You may find more than one, but you will not be truly at home in a new place until you find a heart friend.

In the opening chapter of *Why Am I Afraid to Tell You Who I Am?* Powell quotes the Swiss psychiatrist Dr. Paul Tournier. Tournier says, "It is impossible to overemphasize the immense need humans have to be really listened to, to be taken seriously, to be understood.... No one can develop freely in this world and find a full life without feeling understood by at least one person.... He who would see himself clearly must open up to a confidante freely chosen and worthy of such trust."[2]

Granted, our mate may be that one who understands and listens. But I'm convinced we also need another friend. It is not obligatory that this confidante be a member of your church, *but don't rule out the possibility.*

Regrettably, in the past, ministers' wives were advised never to form close friendships within the local church. I feel sad when I occasionally encounter that philosophy today. About thirty years ago, a pastor's wife said to me, "I never form a close friendship with anyone in the church. It causes jealousy and division. I've seen many ministers' wives betrayed by someone they had trusted. Just take my advice and be pleasant to all but close to none." Interestingly, in that same church a woman expressed a similar philosophy from the layperson's point of view. Her words were, "I never get close to a minister's wife. I did once. Just about the time we became good friends, she moved away. It hurt too much."

I don't believe these two women are representative of most Christians. Thank goodness, I didn't allow these two women to shape my attitudes on friendships!

Much has been written on the pros and cons of developing close, intimate friends within the church family. Even so, I want to add my two cents' worth. Experience has taught me it is possible to have close friends within the church family without creating division in the church. It simply requires some discretion and common sense. "Close friends" does not mean exclusive friends.

Let's get real! Our Lord had special friends. I believe Jesus had a very close, intimate relationship with the family of Mary, Martha, and Lazarus. And how in the world are we to interpret the phrase in John 21:7,20, "the disciple whom Jesus loved," other than an acknowledgement of the special relationship between John and Jesus?

I could no more stop having close friends than I could stop breathing, and often these friends emerge within our church family. I would have shriveled up and died inside without the dear friends in our various churches. They have nurtured, sustained, enriched, and disciplined me as, I trust, I have done in return. These friendships have endured with the passing of time in spite of human imperfections and geographical separation.

We are human, and we will naturally respond to people who are warm and loving and *real*. If someone becomes too possessive, I simply back off a little. In thirty-five years I've had only one church "friend" betray me and only one became so possessive the relationship threatened to smother me. Thank goodness I didn't say, after those two experiences, "Well, no more friendships in the church, it's easier not to get involved emotionally." One of the greatest joys of life in the ministry has been the special friends God sent my way. Why can't ministers' wives allow themselves to be human?

Let God direct you and trust your instincts. A little common sense helps, too! To quote a fellow staff wife, "Be selective when pouring out your heart."

I'm reminded of Proverbs 18:24, "There is a friend who sticks closer than a brother."

One might well ask, after a move, "How do I find such a friend?" Sometimes it really isn't *easy*. A staff wife friend who lives in a highly transient area has struggled to establish even one close relationship. She says that just about the time she begins to form a close friendship, the friend moves away. I have no profound answer, except to advise, "Keep praying for a heart friend. Keep being involved in the lives of others. Keep reaching out to others." We must be available and we must risk openness in order for close friendships to ripen.

Close friendships seldom happen overnight. Only a few times have I experienced an instant rapport with another and had the relationship blossom into a lifelong friendship. You have to work at friendships, much as you have to work at marriage. You have to share experiences and invest time in the relationships.

Seventh, set some new goals, both immediate and

long-term. Write down some things you want to accomplish in the next few weeks or months; and think of at
least one grand, long-range dream you'd like to work
toward. An older staff wife once said to me, "We always
need to have a dream, a goal before us. When we quit
dreaming, we lose our spark, our drive, our zest."

What are your goals for the next year? Maybe they are
as practical as restoring a piece of furniture or getting to
know ten more families at church or inviting your neighbors over for tea. Maybe they are as common among the
sisterhood of women as losing a few pounds or starting a
daily exercise program. (Zack just proofread this chapter
and told me to add: "Maybe your goal, though uncommon, might be making more chocolate pies for your
husband.") Perhaps your goals might include going back
to school, taking a class, starting a career. As for that big,
grand dream, I urge you to have one and keep working
toward it. When God gives us desires and interests, He
gives us abilities for accomplishing those desires. Working
toward goals helps us focus on positives rather than dwell
on unsettling aspects of a move.

Moves have always been gut-wrenching for me. I'm
one of those souls who puts down deep roots wherever I
am. Pulling them up requires radical surgery, but every
move we've made has caused us to grow professionally
and spiritually. Usually, several years have to go by before we can look back and see that growth occurred.
Several times I've had real difficulty recognizing opportunities for growth, such as the time we had to move into
the old, rather grim parsonage! Sometimes our growth
may come from learning to say with Paul, "I've learned
to be content in whatever circumstances I am" (Phil.
4:11).

Starting over is always formidable. The good news is, we don't have to handle it alone! Our Lord really does understand our fears and loneliness during the earthquakes of life, when everything around us is in upheaval.

Making a move is not the only way we are called upon to start over. We have to start over when we enter new phases of life—when the children leave home.

I sat on his smoothly made-up bed, looked at the unnaturally clean room, and fought back the tears. This was the time for which we had reared him—independence. But nothing I told myself made it easy to accept the fact that my firstborn had moved away to college and our family would never again be the same. He would come back from time to time for visits, but the relationship had changed irreversibly, forever. Where had the years gone? It was only a few months ago that I had been engulfed by smelly tennis shoes and hordes of boys in the front yard or in the kitchen, attacking the refrigerator. Now he was six feet two and had driven confidently away to face the world without his mama!

It took me a while to adjust, but, the adjustment was made easier because I had a daughter still at home. I was still needed. There would still be four more years of teenagers around the house, mother/daughter shopping excursions, high school ball games. Then, overnight, she became eighteen, and suddenly she, too, was gone! Zack and I drove home, after taking her to college, to face a house that was disconcertingly quiet.

It's OK to mourn for a short time the ending of the childhood of your children. But we should celebrate their maturing into young adults. We can also celebrate the opportunity to rediscover our mates. Robert Browning knew what he was talking about when he said, "The best is yet to be." How fun it was to experience again the freedom of being just the two of us!

Starting over occurs when we retire.

I'm adjusting to retirement. Mine, not Zack's. After a twenty-five year teaching career, I said good-bye to chalk dust and seventh graders, to lesson plans and twenty-minute lunch breaks. I thought life would be carefree and wonderful! I also said good-bye, though I didn't realize it at the time, to a big part of my identity. For most of my adult life, I had been recognized as "the teacher." It was a title I claimed with pride, being the third generation of females in our family to teach school. My mother's mother had been a pioneer teacher; my mother and father taught collectively for over sixty years; teaching was "in my blood." During the year after I retired, I struggled with an identity crisis, with feelings that I was no longer a productive, useful, significant person.

Whatever thoughts I had about retirement, it seemed our Lord had other thoughts—such as pressuring me to practice the principles suggested in this chapter and opening opportunities for me to teach in many other ways besides school. It seems as though "retire" is not in His vocabulary! I thought I retired in order to enjoy my grandchildren. Zack thinks I retired in order to rediscover the joys of cooking, ironing, and sewing on buttons. Maybe we can negotiate.

Lord, thank you for giving us fields of service. Thank You for special friends. And, help us never to forget You are our best friend, and we never have to move away from You!

10 The Fun Part

Dorothy and I had just come from the matinee of *Annie* and were sitting at an ice cream parlor indulging ourselves in hot fudge sundaes, her choice of refreshment. Her eyes literally sparkled as she talked about the movie. Even though I was a bit tired (it had been a long movie), *she* showed no evidence of slowing down. Her joy and zest for life were so contagious I soon forgot my fatigue.

Listening to her, I was struck by how singularly blessed I was simply to know her. There was always a twinkle in her eye, though this day she was more animated than usual. It was a special occasion. We were celebrating her eighty-ninth birthday!

In that moment, sitting in the little ice cream parlor, it occurred to me, *This is the fun part!* And I wasn't even thinking about the sundaes. What joy it was to experience Dorothy Rainbolt, the special friend I had come to know through church. No matter my circumstance, I was distinctly happier after every occasion to be with Dorothy. She was always positive, always ready with a witty comment.

"Have I told you," she asked with a little chuckle, "about the time I was teaching three-year-olds in Sunday

School? Our memory verse for the day was 'God careth for you.' As I repeated it several times to my little group, emphasizing 'careth,' one little boy said, 'I don't like carrots.' "

Dorothy checked it in here and went on home to be with the Lord at the young age of ninety-three, after blessing my life profoundly. I miss her, but I know heaven has to be even livelier since her arrival!

This book has been about getting to the fun part when you're married to a minister. Actually, that's not something you finally get *to*; it's something you are *in* most of the time if you can only recognize it.

I'm reminded of a recent sermon by my pastor, Dr. Wayne Blankenship. In describing the Christian pilgrimage he said, "The joy is in the journey. Don't miss it by constantly looking forward to a future Utopia." In every church or in every place of service, there will be problems. Mark it down and underscore it with a red line: there will be disappointments and personality conflicts and misunderstandings. If you allow the bad times to devour you, you will miss the fun part. If you'll begin to look for the fun part, you'll likely discover it.

There are many happy by-products of being "in ministry," but the best part, the most joyful part, is *loving people and being loved in return*. Admittedly, one doesn't have to be in "the ministry" to know the joy of loving and being loved. But, we in full-time ministry have the opportunity, perhaps, to come in contact in a more intimate way with more people.

Growing up as I did, it's hardly unusual I would be a people person. My gregarious dad has never met a person he couldn't enjoy talking to and getting to know. Though not quite so quick to strike up an acquaintance with strangers, mother is unsurpassed in her loyalty and devotion and kindness to friends and family. My parents took in a thirteen-year-old foster son when I was a teenager. They often kept the visiting interim pastor in our home on weekends. And since Dad was one of eleven children, and Mother one of four, our country home was always overflowing with aunts and uncles and cousins. Small wonder I always found people interesting and important.

For Zack and me, the fun part began during our first little church when we were invited home with church members for Sunday dinner. I knew it was going to be fun every time someone said, "Ya'll come on over to the house and we'll see if Mama can rustle up sumthin' to eat." Fried chicken, baked ham, roast beef, creamed corn, mashed potatoes, home-canned green beans, fried okra, fruit salad dripping in whipped cream, and two kinds of pie and cake—all in the same meal—was standard fare! Even when there were no screens on the windows and flies could be mistaken for raisins on the cake, it was fun.

The fun part is going with your young husband to summer revival meetings in the country and sitting on hard wood benches at outdoor services, feeling the sweat roll down the back of your dress, fanning with a cardboard fan (donated by the local funeral home), and being so proud of him you think you'll burst when he preaches or sings a solo.

The fun part is when the little church you're serving surprises you with a "money tree" for Christmas, and you know that many of those one-and five-dollar bills pinned on it were given sacrificially. The fun part is being welcomed by a new church with a "pounding" and getting enough sugar and flour and canned goods and homemade jams to last a year.

The fun part is going as a sponsor to church camp and sitting up most of the night talking with teenage girls, listening to their problems, sharing their dreams, and trying to sleep a little on the narrow, squeaky bunk beds. It's even fun when you discover shaving cream between your sheets.

The fun part is when two incorrigible teenagers from your church decide to surprise you on your birthday by showing up at your home with the gift of a live baby pig, which accidentally gets loose in your house. (Upon seeing a sign advertising pigs for sale, they thought, *Wouldn't it be a hoot to take Nancy a pig for her birthday?*) To this day I haven't figured out how to get even with Molly Marshall and Ron Hatley.

The fun part is when young singles stop you on the church parking lot and say, "We need a place to get together tonight after church. Can we bring pizza and come over to your house?" The house is usually a mess, but they don't seem to care.

The fun part is the privilege of serving in churches with some of God's most choice saints—laymen like Allen Wilkinson at Muskogee, who taught us much about hospitality. We were often part of the innumerable groups he hosted at his cabin retreat overlooking the beautiful Illinois River, a place where one felt the presence of God.

The fun part is going back to visit a former church and having people glad to see you even though your husband occasionally ruffled their feathers during your ministry there! It's having people from out of your past continue to telephone and drop by to see you while passing through town. It's receiving letters in annual Christmas cards.

The fun part is going to retreats at conference centers and fellowshipping with some of God's choice servants— missionaries home on furlough, denominational leaders, outstanding preachers, godly laypeople.

The fun part is seeing someone you've counseled find his or her way to victory. It's the opportunity to minister to others and discovering you are receiving more than you're giving. It's getting a note or a telephone call from one who says, "I want to thank you for all you've meant to me," and you don't even realize you've touched that life. It's getting Christmas cards from church members with a little note that says, "We love you."

The fun part is hosting groups of international students in your home and, even though communication is difficult, realizing: we are all alike, with the same needs and hopes. The fun part is getting to know, and having our lives enriched by, those from other nations who have come our way—Moses and Rebecca from Nigeria, Kim (who lived in our home for a while) from Korea, the Chi family from Vietnam, Eduardo from Brazil.

The fun part is discovering that Christians can have fun! Of course, life is often very unfunny, and I never would be flippant about the heartaches of life. Some might ask, "How, in a world so engulfed by suffering and evil, do you dare see humor in life?" I reply, "Perhaps, we cannot afford *not* to. Humor is a gift from God to keep us balanced in an unbalanced world."

The fun part is getting to work more closely with your spouse than most, getting to feel like a team professionally. The fun part is observing the response of others to your mate's leadership and seeing them grow, developing their gifts. The fun part is joining with him in singing duets, or leading conferences, or planning retreats, and feeling a warm glow as you think, 'We really are a team—a good team!'

The fun part is letting yourself be real, genuine, honest. A friend told me a quaint recollection of her grandmother. Whenever her grandmother did the family laundry, the clothes were hung out to dry on three parallel lines behind the house. The line nearest the house stood about a foot higher than the other two lines. Sheets and towels were always hung on the front, higher line in order to hide from view the personal items (such as lingerie and men's underwear) that were hung on the back two lines. Her grandmother wanted to make sure *no one ever saw the personal items.* I'm not suggesting we hang out front all our personal laundry. I *am* suggesting we take off our masks and cease being afraid someone will suspect we possess "underthings" just like everyone else!

The fun part is discovering a minister's wife can become who she was meant to be, not who or what others think she should be, and can serve because she's a child of God, not because she's a minister's wife. The fun part is being married to a wonderful man who encourages me to be me.

In a questionnaire prepared for staff wives, I asked the question, "What special joys and satisfactions have come to you as a result of your being a staff wife?" Here are some of their replies.

• "...the joy of seeing people grow spiritually and having the opportunity to minister both in times of joy and grief."

• "...receiving love and thoughtfulness from people who take the time to show it in special ways. You don't get that in every job."

• "... the lives that have touched me and the relationships that will be eternal. The joy of knowing so many wonderful people far outweighs any sacrifice and far exceeds the monetary gain."

The common thread running through all the responses was *people, relationships, love.*

That's what it's all about. I wouldn't trade it for anything else in the world. I wouldn't trade places with anyone else in the world. So, I guess it's time to admit: God knew what He was about all along when He led Zack Pannell to introduce himself to me during that college choir tour and, pointing to the empty seat beside me, ask, "Do you mind if I sit here?"

I absolutely love the words of the psalmist in Psalm 5:3, "In the morning I will order my prayer to Thee and *eagerly* watch" (author's italics).

Isn't that great? The psalmist couldn't wait to see what God was going to do each day! He started out by praying, then eagerly watched to see what amazing things God would accomplish in and through his life that day. More and more I'm coming to know what the psalmist meant. Every day is a gift. Every day is a day for rejoicing because of Who He is! I can't wait to see what else God has in store for me!

If you know Him, you're one of His called ones. He has called you to serve, and He has called you to enter into a rich and extraordinary fellowship with Him *and* others. If He has let you marry a minister, that's an even greater bonus!

> "O Lord, our Lord, How majestic is Thy name in all the earth, Who hast displayed Thy splendor above the heavens! When I consider Thy heavens, the work of Thy

fingers, The moon and the stars, which Thou hast ordained; What is man, that Thou dost take thought of him? And the son of man that Thou dost care for him? Yet Thou hast made him a little lower than God, And dost crown him with glory and majesty! O Lord, our Lord, How majestic is Thy name in all the earth!''

Heavenly Father, my joy overflows. All I can say is Thank You for letting me serve You. I love You.

DISCUSSION AND STUDY QUESTIONS

Preface
1. Why is there a conflict between meeting perceived expectations and simply being yourself? Explain from your own personal standpoint.
2. Why are most ministers' wives reticent about expressing their true feelings?

Chapter 1
1. Why is serving from a sense of obligation frustrating and spiritually unrewarding?
2. When one realizes that every believer is called, it makes a difference in one's attitude. Why?
3. Give your own definition of holiness. How does Nancy feel about it?
4. Pause to thank God for your calling as well as your husband's.

Chapter 2
1. Is it fair to expect a double standard from your children because of your unique position? Why or why not?
2. List your ideas about how many of the harsh words, tears, and frustrations of parenting could be avoided.
3. What can Nancy mean when she writes: "We can overexpose them [our children] to 'religious acitvity' "?
4. What was Nancy glad about? Talk about her lists of "I wish we had not" and "I wish we had."

Chapter 3
1. Why are so many husbands and wives like "The Odd Couple"?
2. How can misinterpreting the biblical teaching of submission be destructive?
3. If you work outside the home, write down your feelings about your husband's sharing the household duties.
4. List at least seven principles that will enrich one's marriage.

Chapter 4
1. Why is it essential that the staff member's wife determine who she is? Do you really know who you are?
2. What is the first step in finding self?
3. Do church members have a biblical basis for expecting a certain standard of living from the staff wives? If so, why?
4. List the pitfalls in trying to be yourself.
5. Discuss Nancy's suggestions for growing spiritually.

Chapter 5
1. What kind of people are "dragons on the doorstep"?
2. Are dragons ever justified in their "righteous indignation" and criticism?
3. Jot down the positive, biblical ways of dealing with dragons.
4. Ultimately, where should we lay our hurt feelings?
5. Can you recall any times when people were "dragonish" toward you and perhaps you deserved it?

Chapter 6
1. Talk about ways and means of being involved in the world outside your own group.
2. How do you feel about Nancy's relating to Connie? Are there any Connies around you?
3. What does the non-Chrisitan world expect from Christians? Do non-Christians have a right to anticipate such?
4. Name several "fields of harvest."
5. Give your own ideas about why so few Christians are active witnesses.

Chapter 7
1. List Nancy's three options for coping with destructive, negative feelings. Honestly, which option do you generally choose?
2. If you feel another staff member and/or his wife are doing wrong, what would and should you do?
3. Summarize the principles of Philippians 2:3-7. Write them down.
4. Share what you do to help your mate through periods of discouragement.
5. Suggest how staff wives might have more genuine, supportive relationships with one another.

Chapter 8
1. Is "Honey, if you'll just pray about it, you'll feel better," always appropriate?
2. Thoroughly talk about how depression can set in and what to do about it.
3. What did Paul really mean when he counseled, "Rejoice always"?
4. How do you feel about statements like, "Don't worry, be happy no matter what," or even, "This is the happiest day of my life, because my husband is now with the Lord"?
5. Highlight Nancy's principles for getting through the bad, discouraging times.

Chapter 9
1. Explain the trauma of moving from one place of service to another.
2. Elaborate on Author Mary Bess's ideas about the positive aspects of a move.
3. Write down and review Nancy's seven guidelines for making it during the first year on a new "field."

4. What about the idea that the staff couple should have no close friends in the church outside of the staff?

5. What "starting-over" aspects apply when your children leave home?

Chapter 10

1. Spend time talking about the happy by-products of being "in ministry."

2. Write down at least eight of Nancy's "fun parts."

3. If you are in a group, share specific warm feelings about ministry with your husband for the Lord—the joys, the sorrows, the ups, the downs, the caring.

4. This is between God and you. Would you do it all over again?

Notes

Chapter 1
   1. C. S. Lewis, *Surprised by Joy* (San Diego, New York, London: Harcourt Brace Jovanovich, 1955), 191.
   2. J. Harry Cotton and Alexander C. Purdy, "The Epistle to the Hebrews," *The Interpreter's Bible, A Commentary in Twelve Volumes*, Vol. 11, Nolan B. Harmon, ed. (Nashville: Abingdon Press, 1955), 619-620.
   3. Ibid.
   4. Francis W. Beare and Theodore O. Wedel, "The Epistle of the Ephesians," *The Interpreter's Bible, A Commentary in Twelve Volumes*, Vol. 10, Nolan B. Harmon, ed. (Nashville: Abingdon Press, 1955), 682.
   5. Herschel H. Hobbs, "Christians As Ministers," *Studying Adult Life and Work Lessons* (Nashville: Convention Press, July-August-September 1987), 46.

Chapter 3
   1. Elaine Herrin, *When We Say Never* (Nashville: Broadman Press, 1985), 73-79
   2. Richard J. Foster, *Celebration of Discipline* (New York, Hagerstown, San Francisco, London: Harper and Row, Publishers, 1978), 97-98.
   3. Ibid., 107.
   4. Mary E. Bess, *Tips for Ministers and Mates* (Nashville: Broadman Press, 1987), 14.
   5. "How to Stay Married," *Newsweek* (August 24, 1987), 53.
   6. Reprinted by permission from H & L Enterprises, San Diego, California.

Chapter 4
   1. John Powell, *Why Am I Afraid to Tell You Who I Am?* (Niles, Illinois: Argus Communications, 1969), 106.
   2. Ibid., 8.

3. Robert H. Schuller, *Self Esteem: The New Reformation* (Waco, Tex: Word Books, 1982), 48.
4. Ibid., 62.
5. Powell, Ibid., 12.
6. Richard J. Foster, *Celebration of Discipline* (San Francisco: Harper and Row, Publishers, 1978), 15,17.
7. Powell, Ibid., 155.
8. Elizabeth McBurney, "Your Part In Being The Real You." *The Minister's Mate—Two for the Price of One?*, compiled by Terry A. Peck (Nashville: Convention Press, 1986), 134.

Chapter 5
1. Marshall Shelley, *Well-Intentioned Dragons*, (Waco, Tx.: Word Books)

Chapter 6
1. Rebecca Manley Pippert, *Out of the Salt Shaker and Into the World* (Downers Grove, Illinois: Intervarsity Press, 1979).
2. Vonette Bright, *For Such a Time as This* (Old Tappan, New Jersey: Fleming H. Revell Company, 1976), 120-122.
3. Walter Hooper and Owen Barfield, "A Study Guide to *The Screwtape Letters*," *The Screwtape Letters* by C. S. Lewis (Charlotte, North Carolina: Commission Press, 1976), 153.

Chapter 8
1. Charles Swindoll, *Three Steps Forward Two Steps Back* (Nashville: Thomas Nelson Publishers, 1980), 14.
2. Ibid., 17-18.
3. Ibid., 56-57.
4. Paul E. Billheimer, *Don't Waste Your Sorrows* (Minneapolis: Bethany House Publishers, 1977), Chapters 3 and 5.
5. M. Scott Peck, *People of the Lie* (New York: Simon and Schuster, 1983), 123.

Chapter 9
1. Bess, Ibid., 38-39.
2. Powell, Ibid., 1.
3. Karen Hayner, "Your Part In Developing Friendships." *The Minister's Mate—Two for the Price of One?*, compiled by Terry Peck (Nashville, Tennessee: Convention Press, 1986), Chapter 7.